charm Just a lucky guess

Bad luck *I have no luck!*

My lucky day! You make your own luck

BEGINNER'S [illegible]k Hard-luck story

ood luck streak Change your luck

ucky bastard Just a matter of luck *Lucky dog*

next time! My luck has turned Lucky penny

duck ROTTEN LUCK! Lucky charm *Just my luck*

of luck to you! Someone's got to get lucky!

othing to do with it Lucky to be alive!

TA LUCK! Worst luck in the world!

That's good [illegible] ONE [illegible] GOOD LUCK Piece of luck

Pure luck *[illegible]od* [illegible] little luck...

With a[illegible] luc[illegible] *Lucky dog*

You're in lu[illegible]! *Lucky number* Tough luck!

r lucky stars! *kiss for luck* Potluck

Luck

Also by Barrie Dolnick

Minerva Rules Your Future
How to Write a Love Letter (with Donald Baack)
Simple Spells for Hearth and Home
Simple Spells for Success
Simple Spells for Love
The Executive Mystic
Instructions for Your Discontent

Luck

Understanding Luck and Improving the Odds

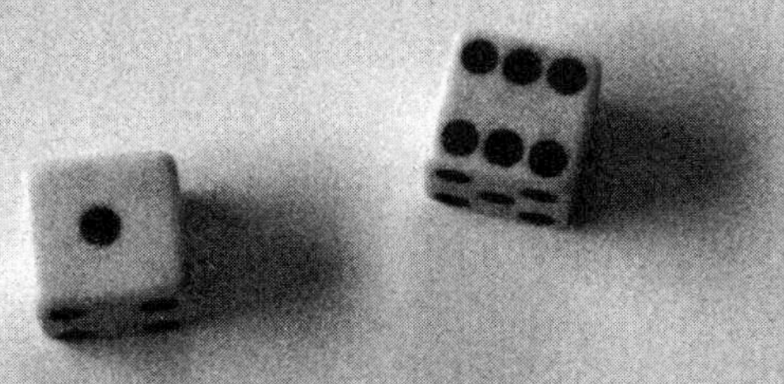

Barrie Dolnick

and

Anthony H. Davidson

Harmony Books

NEW YORK

Published in the United States by Harmony Books, an imprint of the Crown Publishing Group, a division of Random House, Inc., New York.
www.crownpublishing.com

Harmony Books is a registered trademark and the Harmony Books colophon is a trademark of Random House, Inc.

Library of Congress Cataloging-in-Publication Data
Dolnick, Barrie.
Luck : understanding luck and improving the odds / Barrie Dolnick and Anthony H. Davidson.—1st ed.
p. cm.
Includes bibliographical references (p. 231).
1. Fortune. 2. Superstition. I. Davidson, Anthony H. II. Title.
BF1778.D65 2007
131—dc22 2007013235

ISBN 978-0-307-34750-3

Printed in the United States of America

Design by Lynne Amft

10 9 8 7 6 5 4 3 2 1

First Edition

This book is dedicated to our families and to anyone who has ever given someone a lucky break

Acknowledgments

I wish to thank my coauthor, Barrie Dolnick, who saw the potential in this idea and helped make it happen. I am grateful to my wife, Sheila, and my sons, Andrew and Patrick, for being tolerant and supportive of a new creative process. I also thank my family, Dad (Phil), Mom (Pat), Barb, Merry and Charlie, Tom and Joan, Wendy and Todd, and Phil and Lindsay, for keeping our family luck flowing. Thanks to Alan Nevins for his help and Shaye Areheart for her expertise. And to luck, which comes in many forms, in many ways, in all our lives.

A.D.

Deepest gratitude is due to Tony Davidson for his persistence, his vision, and his intellectual contributions—this was his idea. I am so grateful as always to Gero and Elisabeth for their understanding and respect while I write; to my mom and sisters, who keep me laughing; and to my friends Cheryl, Christine, Joelle, and Sheila, who celebrate luck in all its forms. I am also particularly grateful to Sabrina Diano for her friendship and help in translation, and to Professor Kathryn Shanley, who brought medicine into my life. Thanks to Alan Nevins and his sharp eye for the right track and to Shaye Areheart, who is more than an editor—she's a true friend.

B.D.

Contents

Part Two: Personal Luck Profile

Preface

What happens when you ask someone for a concrete opinion about the existence of or belief in luck? We asked ourselves that question.

Luck is a vast subject that is extremely personal. It's like God or the existence of a soul: You believe in it, maybe you toy with believing in it, or you just dismiss it as unworthy of your time. It can evoke a broad spectrum of feelings, ranging from enthusiasm (generally from those who feel lucky) to annoyance and frustration. No one can deny that there are situations in which luck plays a big role. No one can avoid using the word *luck* in everyday language. It seems to be as embedded in our lives as breathing.

So why do we want to write about luck? We have several motivations. We want to examine luck in its historical context. We want to see if it is possible to understand it better. We want to use it in our lives. We want to form an opinion about luck that we can share with you.

We are interested in exploring luck on behalf of the public. Luck is courted openly by millions of people who play lotteries and go to casinos. Luck is silently wished for and prayed for when business deals are proposed, ball games are played, and parking spaces are sought. We talk about luck all the time. We wish it for our friends and neighbors and certainly hope to capture some for ourselves.

PART ONE

Examining Luck

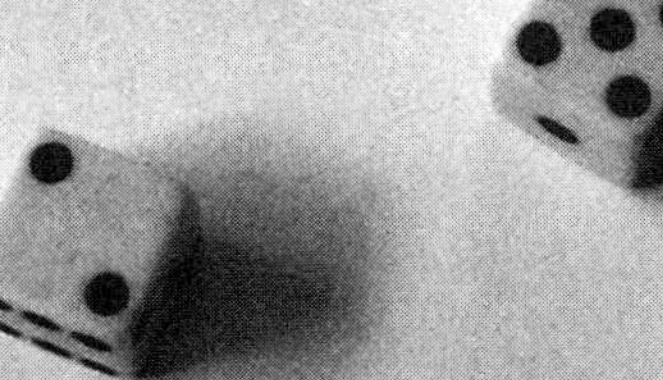

We are all too ready to forget that in fact everything to do with our life is chance, from our origin out of the meeting of spermatozoon and ovum onwards.

—Sigmund Freud

Chapter 1

Luck Begins

You very likely utter this word at least once a day without even thinking about it. Luck.

"Bye—and good luck," you say, ending a phone call.

"I got lucky," you think when you snag a great parking space.

"She's so lucky," you think when you hear about a friend who got a better job.

You live with luck as your silent companion for your whole life. Most of the time, you probably don't even pay attention to it. Chances are, you really think about luck only when you buy a lottery ticket or participate in a contest.

Luck is so much more than that.

Superstition? Luck? What's the Difference?

The interweaving themes of luck and superstition are so knotted over time that it's almost impossible to separate them. Yet we want you to notice a slight difference.

According to Dictionary.com, **luck** (as a noun) is:

THE FORCE THAT SEEMS TO OPERATE FOR GOOD OR ILL IN A PERSON'S LIFE, AS IN SHAPING CIRCUMSTANCES, EVENTS, OR OPPORTUNITIES.

Superstition is:

A BELIEF OR NOTION, NOT BASED ON REASON OR KNOWLEDGE, IN OR OF *THE OMINOUS SIGNIFICANCE* OF A PARTICULAR THING, CIRCUMSTANCE, OCCURRENCE, PROCEEDING, OR THE LIKE.

Luck is defined as a force that tips the balance in life. Superstition is merely a belief or idea based on "nothing" to alleviate fear or harm. Forget superstition—let's study luck and see if this force can be understood.

For our purposes, we define luck as winning in the short term or being successful in the long term owing to chance.

Does Luck Exist?

From the philosophical perspective, luck exists because often we lack complete information and perfect predictive powers. If an event is uncertain and the result is positive, it can be attributed to good luck.

Is Luck a Force of Nature?

We think so. It is certainly a part of human nature. The belief in luck is somewhat similar to the belief in God. It takes faith that it exists.

We've seen luck appear in the most unusual circumstances. It intervenes, like grace, in situations where even hope is fading. What differs is that luck can appear even when you don't need it. Luck is just one of those things in life that you either acknowledge and work with or ignore and deny. It is there whatever you do.

We have written this book to reacquaint you with the concept of luck and to help you develop a relationship with it. What is luck? Why is it sometimes defined through a horseshoe or a four-leaf clover? What's been lucky in the past, and what might be lucky in the future? Are some people born lucky? Can you improve your own luck?

The history of luck is extensive and fascinating. The belief in luck began with the most ancient cultures—as early as cavemen. We have found that our ancestors studied the subject carefully, and much of what they found and believed survives today.

Is luck something we can understand? Is it just superstitious to assume we can attract luck? We've examined the issue from many angles, and we've come to believe that although you can't control luck, you can certainly understand it and explore your relationship with luck effectively. We believe that there are luckier times in our lives and that it's possible to forecast when luck will be with us. We also think that knowing when your luck is "out" is even more interesting—those are the "walk away and don't take risks" periods when you don't have luck working for you.

How people see luck these days is varied and personal. Yet no one, not even the most hard-core rationalist, is immune from using the word *luck* or judging something or someone to be lucky. Luck is embedded in our consciousness, if not our DNA.

Where do you start with luck? It's tough to approach such a huge topic. To get an idea of how the concept of luck takes root in society, we thought we'd just look around. In the short history of the United States, it is fascinating to see how luck worked its way through the melting pot. Our brief survey of luck in America provides a fast-forwarded summary of how luck is seen through the eyes of different people.

The history of luck itself is also curious. Since the belief in luck seems as ancient as humans, we went back in time as far as we could. We found that luck originates with nature itself. Abundance, prosperity, health, triumph—these were and still are the needs, wants, and wishes of all men and women. But the natural world was chaotic and unpredictable, which is precisely why the ancients studied it for its links and clues to luck and good fortune. To understand nature was to interpret its signs. Good luck is grounded in the natural world, and we examine some ancient luck symbols that are still found today.

These symbols of luck are as simple as acorns and dolphins. Luck in the natural world is about animals, plants, and minerals that became, through experience, associated with prosperity and health and therefore luck. Certain symbols also took on meaning, such as the horseshoe. Once you understand how these symbols became lucky, you can decide whether they are indeed relevant to your luck.

From the natural world, ancient people became more sophisticated with interpretation and advanced methods for prediction and forecasting. In some societies, divination was a part of spiritual practice. In other cultures, predictions were simply like farm reports or policy advice. The best advisers to kings, emperors, chiefs, and leaders, and in some cases the leaders themselves, devised ways to predict the future so that they could anticipate and plan for events. In examining luck, it is important to follow these ancient roads that determined today's major forms of divination. History is filled with instances where divinations correctly predicted events. The sighting of a comet was interpreted to predict the assassination of the Roman emperor Claudius; he was poisoned soon after. Bad luck and good luck might be predictable. We cover astrology, the oldest science, and numerology—very important in identifying lucky numbers—as well as the I Ching (developed by an emperor), tarot, palmistry, and even tea leaf reading. It is truly amazing to witness how cultures around the world developed methods to predict future events and therefore prepare for good luck or bad luck.

After you gain a better understanding of luck over the ages, some of your curiosity might be satisfied. Maybe you'll find that you now understand why your grandmother always had nutmeg or hung a horseshoe. Having perspective of where traditional luck beliefs come from can free you to either use it or toss it. You'll be able to make choices about luck just from understanding a bit about its history.

From this subjective perspective on luck, we'll move into a more rational framework. Great mathematicians, many of whom were avid gamblers, developed mathematical theories that contributed to our knowledge of luck. While no mathematician provides key evidence to prove good luck or bad luck, some have given us a chance to see "how much luck is needed" to win in a given situation. Much of their work is used every day in gambling and games of chance, not just in the classroom. Of course, mathematicians are only human, and they did what they could to improve their own chances of winning.

Nowhere is luck courted more openly and more often than in gambling. Gross gambling revenue in the United States is reported to be over $84 billion. Almost everyone in the country is offered a chance to enter a sweepstakes, buy a lottery ticket, or enter a casino. States rely on gambling revenues for operating budgets. Since luck has a great deal to do with gambling (skill plays a role, but luck is always the final word), we address games of chance in a dedicated chapter. Our experience and study provide an explanation not only of the most popular games, but also of the odds of winning and how much luck you need to win. It is here that the mathematical information will come in handy. We also give you eight rules of luck to help you get lucky in gambling and risk taking in other parts of your life.

Finally, no book about luck would be complete without a tribute to the wacky things people do for luck. From wearing lucky pajamas (passed down from one champ to another) to carrying weird objects, these stories make us smile and, perhaps, wonder if that stuff might just work for us. Johnny Chan and Doyle Brunson, the only living men to twice win the World Series of Poker held at Binion's Horseshoe Casino in Las Vegas, are both known for lucky objects.

Entertaining, perhaps inspiring, these stories of luck and lucky charms will make you think twice about what you're doing about your own luck.

That's where the second part of the book will help. We have established some diagnostic information so that you can predict your lucky cycles. You'll be able to use some of the tools we present in earlier chapters and apply them to create your personal luck profile. We also provide more information on lucky herbs, stones, colors, and other details that you may want to try on your own.

By giving you some strong sense of how luck has been tracked and understood through the millennia, we hope that you can use this information in your own life to enrich your experience, if not your bank account.

From our own research, we have enjoyed a great deal of new information and even some sense—if luck permits the use of the word—of how to cope with and understand how luck works. The gambler looking for luck at the craps table who cries out, "God, give me money!" attracts the wise counsel of his fellow gamblers: "God has nothing to do with money." That might be true. But luck does care about money, and so do most of us. Luck, however, isn't just about cash. Luck helps with health, love, and abundance in many forms. God might help with that as well, but luck is perhaps a creation of God that gives us a little something to play with. Luck keeps us surprised.

So let's play.

I think that Americans, of all the nationalities, most profoundly believe in luck. We began as a nation by gambling on the future of a continent. Most of our great industrial pioneers have been inspired gamblers. We are the three-card monte men of the world. We have roulette wheels spinning in our brains, and anything is likely to turn up.

—William Rose Benét

Chapter 2

Luck in Our Own Backyard

In a *New York Times* review of new television game shows, Alessandra Stanley opens her article with the following assertion:

> *Game shows are not quiz shows. That should be understood at the outset, because knowledge is not an American virtue; luck is.*

Television both reflects our culture and shapes it. Today's game shows give us a glimpse into our own relationship with luck. We watch others test their luck to see how tolerant we would be as luck gets pushed again and again. Game shows are popular staples of radio and television, but we can dial back a few centuries, way before television, and catch the beginning of America's delight in playing with luck.

America's Brand of Luck

American luck began with Native American culture, thriving thousands of years before the first English settlers came to eastern shores. Since then, American luck has been shaped by waves of Western European immigration and the influence of Africans who came as slaves, as well as by people with diverse cultures from around the world who have come to live in the "melting pot" of America. To catch a glimpse of American luck, we can flip through the pages of history. There are many contributors who have shaped our attitude toward luck today, but we pluck only a few of these contributions to give you a sense of how luck rules so much of our cultural heritage. While we glance through history, keep in mind the elements that contribute to a belief in luck.

Native Americans	Puritans/ Colonists	African slaves	French/ Spanish West settled	Industrial-ization	WWI/ WWII

<_________1600______1700_____1800_______1900_________>2000

Throughout American history, luck has been shaped by multicultural influences and basic human nature.

Native American Luck: Nature Rules

Native Americans are a diverse group of tribal nations that in general defy a blanket cultural definition. There are over five hundred distinct groups across the country, most of which differ in language, tribal culture, and history. However, certain broad strokes are clear: Nature and spirituality are intertwined, and a profound belief in luck is common throughout tribal cultures. Luck is spirit; there is no separation.

Luck was in many cases defined as "medicine" derived from the connection between the spirit world and the physical world. "Medicine" means mystery, sensibility, power, and influence—a connection to the spirit world. Luck was medicine that brought people together and ensured prosperity and harmony for the tribe.

The medicine man (who can also be a woman) is something of a holy person who is designated as such by the tribe. He or she typically apprentices with an elder to learn by oral tradition and hands-on experience. The gift of medicine, however, is also found among other tribe members. He or she is a person who understands nature and messages of the spirit world.

Professor Kathryn Shanley (Assiniboine/Nakota), chair of the Department of Native American Studies at the University of Montana, asserts that in twentieth-century Plains Indian literature, luck appears as "a metaphysical concept; roughly described, it is a 'portal' to the spiritual realm where power—better termed 'medicine'—can be obtained."

All tribe members could be given medicine in dreams. Luck was tied to omens that came in strong dream scenarios that were shared among the tribe. Members would acquire names and positions from their dream scenarios. Sometimes dreams were induced by herbs or by spiritual journeys in coming-of-age rituals. It was so important to have medicine dreams that luck would actually turn for the better after someone had a medicine dream.

Medicine was—and still is—administered through herbs, rituals, and songs. You can find Native American gambling songs, gaming songs, and even something called "Geronimo's Medicine Song" on the Internet. Chanting and the power of word and sound are ways to attract luck and strong medicine.

MEDICINE IN NATURE

For the Sioux, Zuni, and Dakota tribes, the number 4 was sacred. Four was a number that held the power of the universe, the seasons, the four directions—and the nature of good luck.

Various good-luck symbols in Native American culture included rain clouds, raindrops, and buffalo. A fence symbol guarded good luck, and a mountain symbol stood for abundance. The herbs avens and fuzzy weed were used by Native Americans for luck in love, meadow rue for protection, and yellow evening primrose for luck in hunting. Sagebrush was and is still used to drive away negative forces so that good influences can thrive.

You might be familiar with Zuni Pueblo Indian fetishes. This tribe associates different powers with animals. The medicine bear stands for good luck. Today, there are many Native American fetishes, animal charms, dolls, and symbols that are used to attract wisdom and luck. The roots of luck in North America come distinctly from nature.

NATIVE GAMES

Gambling was also popular among tribes, and many games of chance were passed down through the generations.

The Algonquins, a tribe that spanned most of the country's northern territory, has a deep tradition that links gambling with games of the spirits. Spirits are playing with your fate in any gambling game—if the spirits are doing well, your luck and life will go well. If you have a powerful gambler above, your life will have good luck. You live with the consequences of the game that the spirits are playing.

Playing with luck is pervasive and continues today, albeit more profitably, with casinos on tribal land.

Native American culture brings three important themes to the surface. First, nature plays a huge role in defining what is lucky and what is not. Second, information about luck is derived through divination and prediction. Third, playing with luck through gambling was an important and often spiritual pastime. Luck is a strong thread in the fabric of Native American culture. Europeans arrived in America with a different idea—yet you'll see that nature, divination, and gambling emerge again in America's experience with luck.

Even Puritans Couldn't Resist a Peek into Luck

As you probably know, the first Europeans to settle in what is now the United States were the Puritans, a group who left England to escape religious persecution. The Puritans sought simple lives away from corruptive influences like drinking, gambling, breaking the Sabbath, and other sins of society. Puritans faced a tough life in the New World, and their future was all too uncertain. To avoid looking superstitious, they used the Bible to help make decisions—to indicate where luck would be found. Would there be enough food for winter? Would there be illness or health in the house? The Bible was consulted. This method—turning to a random page for a word or phrase for guidance or gentle prediction—is called bibliomancy. Although religious leaders did not support it, this form of divination was part of family life and culture.

Native Americans believed in luck openly. Puritans were uncomfortable with anything outside of God's word. Puritans used bibliomancy to give insight to luck.

Raising a Colony on a Lottery

Non-Puritans also settled in North America and brought more lenient views of luck to society. Lotteries were actually used by the British company that financed the Jamestown colony to help raise its venture capital. The colonists loved to gamble and to play with luck. It seems that the chance to get rich quick was part of early American dreams.

Games of chance grew more common as the population grew in the seventeenth century. Although there were several laws banning lotteries, fortune-telling, cards, and dice throughout the first thirteen colonies, gambling still found a place in society. Betting on horses grew popular in Virginia's horse country. Virginians were also less strict about ancient tools like herbal magic, astrological readings, and magical practices, and many held on to "fortune books" that gave insight into luck.

Gambling for sport was prevalent in the colonies. So was divination. Nature's influence over luck was found in things like coral, which was supposed to bolster a child's health. Although separate from Native Americans in their beliefs about luck, Colonial Americans connected to luck along similar lines.

Rosicrucians, the Birth of the United States, and Luck

When the colonists decided to break away from England, our Founding Fathers thoughtfully employed symbols and images that would enhance the luck of the new nation. Thomas Jefferson and Benjamin Franklin were members of a secret order of Rosicrucians, who believed (among other things) in the power of numbers and symbols. While the Rosicrucians were sensitive to attention and under scrutiny by churches, their ranks included many influential and powerful men who shaped the young country. William Penn, founder of Pennsylvania, was another early American who was active in Rosicrucian society and championed America's religious freedom. You'll see lasting imprints of the Rosicrucians on American currency: A "third eye" as well as a pyramid underline divine mystery and power.

As the Declaration of Independence was signed, the Sibley brothers of London, famous astrologers, cast the horoscope for the country so that its fortune and destiny could be studied. Although Europe was, at the time, more inclined toward scientific and rational explorations, fortunes and destinies were still being analyzed through the stars. While it is argued that the Sibleys' chart of the country contained errors, it has been consulted and reworked ever since it was cast—and continues to be used by astrologers to forecast the fortunes of the United States.

African Americans and the Powers of Luck

Another important layer to America's roots of luck is derived from the population of Africans who came to North America as slaves, some as early as the first settlers. Drawn from all over the African continent, this population brought diverse beliefs in magic, spirituality, and luck. As Africans arrived in greater numbers in the early 1700s, their beliefs began to blend with Native American and European concepts.

Africans arrived in the New World with strong spiritual practices and beliefs. As with Native Americans, there were many peoples and different customs.

One example of an African contribution to a uniquely American belief in luck is the Seven African Powers, derived from a spiritual connection to nature. These powers are invoked in hoodoo practice and bring luck, power, and protection. According to hoodoo expert Catherine Yronwode, these powers can be traced to West Africa's Yoruba tribe and their original spiritual practice. This tribe's three-tiered concept of one creator God, a realm of messenger spirits, and a realm of spirits of the dead was melded into more Christian terms—the creator God became Jehovah, and the numerous messengers of the second tier became angels. Spirits of the dead became equated with saints. In vastly abbreviated terms, the Yoruba's tribal beliefs became defined as the Seven African Powers. What had been a spiritual practice of some African people got reshaped, reinterpreted, and in some ways force-fitted into a form more attuned to American beliefs.

In more recent years, the Seven African Powers have been sold as a magical formula. African slaves also brought us the concept of "spirit bundles" for luck and protection.

A Word on Hoodoo

Hoodoo is a term that encompasses almost every kind of ritual magic, herbal bundling, symbols, and fortune-telling that exists. Hoodoo is *not* voodoo. Rather, hoodoo is complicated ritual magic that draws from numerous cultures and requires study, expertise, and respect. Whatever you think, hoodoo's core connects to ancient beliefs in power and luck.

Hoodoo is magical practice that lays a strong foundation for American luck beliefs today. High John the Conqueror root is one of the most common herbs for luck in hoodoo. This root is extremely strong (it is literally very hard) and can be carried in a pocket or spirit bundle to bring good luck or power.

Hoodoo is probably more common in the southern United States, particularly in New Orleans, which once was home to famous practitioners. However, today's lucky charms, lucky stones, and even rituals of luck derive from this cultural blend. You might not call it hoodoo, maybe you call it mojo—whatever it is, it's all around you.

New Frontiers for Luck in the Wild West

As the United States grew in population and development pushed westward, the spirit of exploration and freedom was a great breeding ground for games of chance and tests of luck. Riverboat gambling described by Mark Twain preceded the great Gold Rush of 1849 in California. It's said that the people who got really lucky out there were the ones selling the shovels. Luck comes in all forms.

The Gold Rush of the mid-1800s was all about trying your luck. Luck was right there in nature in the form of precious gold. Just when the spirit of the 49ers was flagging, the Comstock Lode—the largest silver lode in the United States—was discovered in Nevada, giving this state its nickname, the Silver State. The chance for fortune was contagious in the West, and over seventeen thousand people ran to join the silver miners.

Where there is money, there are always people trying to get lucky.

The 1800s was also the period made famous by legendary gamblers Diamond Jim Brady, John Henry "Doc" Holliday, and Wild Bill Hickok. Lucky objects played a role in these times, but people didn't have many possessions on the frontier. A man might have had a lucky hat, certainly not a new hat (which was unlucky), and it was considered bad luck to put a hat on a bed.

Americans Love to Play

The love of playing with luck no doubt contributed to the invention of the first slot machine later in the 1880s, but it wasn't until 1931 that gambling was legalized in Nevada (not that gambling or games of chance needed legality to be played). In less than three hundred years, America's love of playing with luck grew as fast as its population. The bold, adventurous energy of western expansion across the continental United States fed the country's appetite for luck and fortune. The American dream became much more than the "work hard and it pays off" Puritan work ethic. Taking a chance, making bold moves, and the spirit of enterprise were just as important. Risk was fun. It was okay to dream of winning a lottery or investing in a newfangled idea. Even if there was nothing to explore, no gold or silver to mine, and no casinos in which to gamble, the pursuit of luck was alive and well in America.

The Policy Game, Dreaming of Luck

You might have heard of "running the numbers" or "bolita," both of which are names for the policy. First invented in Chicago and soon rampant across the country, this illegal betting game allowed anyone to put down a small amount of money on numbers in combination from 2 to 25. A wheel was spun, numbers "won," and those who bet on those numbers got a payout. Policy offered everyone a chance to win big in theory, but in practice most games were prone to corruption. State lotteries and Powerball have replaced policy today, but the desire to win big, play for luck, and take a chance on a number is the same as it was back then.

The policy game gave players a chance to consider lucky numbers and play certain combinations that were meaningful to the individual. A birthday or a wedding day was an easy pick. However, people looked for more than just the obvious numbers to guide them to a win. An entire industry developed around identifying numbers for good luck. African American writer Claude McKay said, "Harlem was set upon a perpetual hunt for lucky numbers."

The most famous book on luck in the United States from this era is called *Aunt Sally's Policy Players Dream Book.* From the 1890s through the 1940s, people turned to books that interpreted dream symbols into numbers. Dream books like these can be found in African culture as well as French and Italian.

In each case, you would take your dream from the night before and look up its symbols for the assigned numerical meaning. If you dreamed about a cat, the number 14 had something to do with your fortune. But it doesn't stop at that point. Your dream symbols could be both omens and numbers, and it was up to you to decide what it meant (with the help of a dream book).

Dreams are often considered important clues for luck. Dreams gave medicine to many Native Americans. Dream symbols meant numbers to the policy game players.

The dream books were so commonplace that a hit song of 1901 memorialized them. "Four-Eleven-Forty-Four" was a three-number "gig" that was popular in policy. This number sequence appeared on the cover of *Aunt Sally's Policy Players Dream Book.*

Twentieth-Century Luck

By 1912, the United States comprised forty-eight continental states. There was continuing vigor in economic enterprise and the "good old American way of life." Luck turned, however, in 1917, when the United States officially entered World War I. Never before was luck more necessary. In this "war to end all wars," soldiers needed whatever they could to get through the battlefield alive. With battles in the air, land, and sea—and vicious new weapons including mustard gas, chlorine gas, and torpedoes—soldiers did what they could to protect themselves. At the time, the swastika, a symbol derived from the Sanskrit word for good fortune, was employed by the 45th Infantry Division on shoulder patches during the war. In World War II, the 45th Infantry Division abandoned the swastika because of the Nazis and instead adopted the Native American symbol of the thunderbird.

At the end of World War I, the economy boomed, the 1920s roared in, and gambling (known in more genteel circles as "speculation") in the stock market reached manic proportions. Again, luck was pushed in a truly American fashion. Luck turned, and the stock market crashed.

In these bleak economic times, lucky objects differed by region. There were lucky beans, lucky buttons, and lucky glass. People warded off bad luck by charms or protective amulets. You can still buy 1930s lucky coins.

In 1939, *Pot O' Gold* debuted, the first game show in which a money giveaway was a central theme. To win, a listener would have to be home to answer the phone in order to win $1,000. This was just the beginning of a long history in media in which games of chance attract large audiences.

As World War II escalated in the 1940s, luck once again was called for on the battlefield. Airmen painted lucky symbols on the noses of their aircraft—from winning poker hands to dice throws and four-leaf clovers. Some art was as elaborate as it was meaningful. "Superstitious Aloysius," a happy little gnome carrying a wishbone, was often found on the noses of airplanes.

It must be noted that the war was won, in part, because of Native American luck. Navajo code talkers confounded the Japanese and were able to communicate securely throughout the Pacific front. The code talkers participated in a Navajo Blessingway ceremony before departing for their service. The Blessingway ceremony incorporates song to ensure good luck and good health. Native American luck played a role in twentieth-century warfare.

Luck Today

Postwar America was a time of great industrial and commercial expansion. The 1950s and 1960s were economic boom times. Casinos blossomed in the Nevada desert. Gambling was legalized in Atlantic City in 1978. In the 1980s, the Supreme Court ruled that Native American tribes could own and operate casinos on their land. This has changed the face of gaming in the United States and has made playing with luck more accessible than ever.

> *Native American luck was about spiritual connection. Today, luck is about winning money.*

Flip on today's top-rated shows and you'll see games of chance. *Deal or No Deal* on NBC is soon to be joined by more shows based on pure luck. On *Deal or No Deal,* contestants pick from twenty-six briefcases for a chance to win $1 million or more. Contestants use lucky numbers, lucky cards, lucky shirts, lucky people—anything they think will bring them luck. Ratings soared as the jackpot was pushed up to $10 million on a season opener. The very soul of this show is luck. Studio and home audiences cannot suppress their desire to see how far the contestant will go. In some respects, viewers are luck voyeurs. Playing with luck is a thrill in both anticipation and winning. Losing, on the other hand, is painful.

Games of chance are also a favorite of churches (bingo) and governments (lotteries and off-track betting). Playing with luck has become an attractive and economical way to raise funds. Playing with luck is embedded in our culture.

Summing Up

A quick trip through American history gives a glimpse into the development of luck as a society grows more complex. Starting with Native Americans, dream medicine, and herbal powers, adding puritanical bibliomancy, games of chance, and lucky objects in the new colonies, plus the influx of African Americans who brought influential beliefs in spirits and powers of luck, and finally the westward push and great fortunes manifested overnight with gold and silver strikes: This is the foundation of the desire to "get rich quick" and how it emerged as the American dream. Luck appears to permeate every step. Luck is found in nature and in dreams; luck is conjured in hoodoo and guided by lucky objects. Nature, divination, and gambling are all sources of American luck.

Most of what the United States has experienced in the last several hundred years has been taking place all over the globe for thousands of years. We now explore how luck has been examined, defined, analyzed, and molded through the ages.

Why go further and further,
Look, happiness is right here.
Learn how to grab hold of luck,
For luck is always there.

—JOHANN WOLFGANG VON GOETHE

Chapter 3

Luck and the Natural World

The foundation of luck is in nature, and ancient civilizations relied on clues from nature to anticipate good fortune. Human nature looked for links, clues, and connections to be prepared for the future. When a link between luck and nature was suspected, the belief was passed down through generations. An acorn was associated with an oak tree, the tree many ancient people connected with wisdom and protection. The acorn is still a symbol of luck and fertility (often the same thing in historical context) and is seen throughout talismans and amulets as well as arts and crafts. Symbols of luck have endured for generations.

Have you ever considered why these symbols endure? Why is a four-leaf clover or a rabbit's foot supposed to be lucky? The reason things are held to be lucky varies, but it is almost always because of our love of life and staying healthy, the desire for abundance, and the wish for love and a happy romance.

Health, money, and love: Luck plays a leading role in all three. Here we present what thousands of years of experience reveals about what brings us luck.

A World of Experience with Animals, Plants, Minerals, and Symbols

Lucky symbols and objects are found among animals, plants, and minerals. In our investigations, it was interesting to see how many different cultures came up with similar beliefs about good luck. You'll see many familiar things here, but the reason things are lucky might surprise you. There are more exhaustive lists for good-luck symbols from the natural world in the "Personal Luck Profile" section. We suggest you read through the following descriptions so that you see the relationship between good-luck symbols and their historical context. You might be surprised how often you carry on traditions of luck without even knowing it.

Here are some more famous selections from around the world that illustrate how nature plays a strong role in what we consider lucky.

ANIMALS

Bats

Bats are considered lucky in Chinese culture. The word for "bat" sounds the same as the word *fu,* which means "good fortune" in Chinese. Five red bats (made from paper) are exceptional good luck because the color red and the number 5 are both lucky. The Japanese and the Poles also think that a bat is a sign of long life and good fortune. Some Greeks consider bat bones to be lucky and carry a small bit of the bone in their pockets. Other Greeks think a bat is unlucky on any occasion. In any case, they agree it's bad luck to kill a bat.

The Beckoning Cat

You have seen these cats in Asian restaurants and businesses, a cat with raised forepaws, known as "the beckoning cat." The cat is placed in windows and in prominent positions because it brings good luck. The cat is often wearing red, a good-luck color. The cat's luck is linked to a Japanese samurai story where a cat guided a wealthy warrior to a poor monastery, where the monks taught him Buddhism. The monastery became prosperous. The beckoning cat brings abundance by attracting patrons to come into businesses.

Carp and Goldfish

In Eastern cultures, goldfish and their bigger cousins carp are considered lucky not just for the color of abundance, but for their strength and ability to survive. They can grow large and live very long given the right conditions. They are a symbol of abundance in a home.

Dolphins

Many eastern Mediterranean people believe that dolphins are lucky. Again, luck and wealth seem to be tied together, since dolphins drive fish into nets, increasing the catch and wealth of the fishermen. The dolphin symbol can be seen on amulets and mixed with other lucky symbols all around the world. Among the cultures that have esteemed dolphins are the Maoris of New Zealand, natives of the Amazon region, Native Americans, Celts, and Greeks.

Elephants

The people of India believe that elephants are sacred and lucky. An elephant with its trunk turned upward stores good luck. An elephant with its trunk turned downward dispenses good luck. In feng shui, it is believed that a pair of elephants with their trunks up by the front door of the household will bring good fortune and strength.

Frogs

Germans consider frogs a good-luck symbol in business because frogs can go only forward, not backward.

The Japanese believe that frogs are good luck in part because they produce a vast number of eggs (1,500 at a time). Fertility is a sign of abundance and good luck. The Japanese word for frog is *kaeru,* which sounds phonetically like the words for "return money" or "return good fortune."

In Chinese culture today, the frog, often seen as a statue with a gold coin in its mouth, is still associated with riches. The Chinese also revered Chan Chu, the toad god, as a symbol of good luck, especially in business. The toad is lucky because it is capable of transformations.

In ancient Egypt, frogs were so important that the Egyptians sometimes put frog figures on a mummy to promote rebirth of the dead.

It's interesting that the Old Testament cites frogs as one of the ten plagues of Egypt in the story of Exodus. An old superstition holds that killing a frog brings bad luck.

Ladybugs

Americans and Europeans believe that if a ladybug lands on you and flies away, it's good luck. In Canada, people make a wish, and whichever direction the ladybug flies away is where the wish will come from. Central Europeans and some Swedes believe that if a ladybug crawls across a maiden's hand, she will soon be married. In England, each spot on a ladybug means a lucky month to come.

Monkeys

Monkeys are considered lucky in Chinese culture. The monkey is one of the major animals in Chinese astrology. In casinos throughout the world, Chinese gamblers often say the word *monkey* after placing a bet to summon good luck.

Pigs

Germans believe in "lucky pigs." Legend has it that the Teutons sacrificed pigs to the gods for good luck. There is no doubt that this belief is tied to the use of piggy banks. In Germany, when someone is lucky, it is customary to say, *Ich habe Schwein gehabt,* which means "I have had pig." You might recall once telling someone they were a "lucky pig." Now you know why.

Rabbits

Rabbits are a universally accepted good-luck symbol. A rabbit's luck is tied to its fertility, historically linked to abundance. Farmers wanted to have big families to help with the fields. Noblemen wanted to have sons to carry on the family fortune and daughters to marry and extend family alliances. Historically, fertility was linked directly to prosperity and therefore luck. The rabbit was also a favorite animal of the Greek goddess of love, Aphrodite, again a symbol of fertility. African slaves believed that carrying the foot of a fast animal would bring luck in escape. Some believe that the lucky rabbit's-foot charm is derived from slave culture.

Scarabs

The people of Egypt believe that the scarab or good-luck beetle protects from harm and brings good luck. This good-luck symbol has been around for over four thousand years. Its longevity is part of the reason it brings good luck.

PLANTS

People throughout time have used plants for attracting luck, as exemplified by Native American culture and how roots and herbs were used for good medicine. The plant world offers an abundance of food and healing properties, but botanical luck is derived from ancient cultural symbolism, beyond use just for food and headache cures.

Acorns

Norsemen consider acorns lucky. Acorns are a symbol of rebirth and regeneration. Norse customs call for acorns to be placed on windowsills to protect the house from lightning. As a vestige of this custom, curtains and blinds often have an acorn attached to the rod or at the end of the pull.

Druids in what is now northern France and Britain worshipped in groves of oak trees and believed the acorn to be a strong symbol of power and luck.

Acorns, like most nuts, are considered good luck for fertility as well. A nut is a seed, and a seed will germinate and form new life. If you want to get pregnant, it is supposed to be good luck to eat lots of seeds and nuts. Similarly, the acorn is a symbol of prosperity. Slip an acorn into your pocket and see if it brings you luck.

Bamboo

In Eastern cultures, bamboo is considered a good-luck plant and is a great housewarming gift. Feng shui experts consider bamboo lucky when it is given with all five elements: wood, earth, water, fire, and metal.

Wood—the plant.
Earth—what the plant lives in.
Water—use to keep the plant alive.
Fire—red that should decorate the planter.
Metal—a coin that sits at the base of the bamboo.

Cabbage and Black-Eyed Peas

Associated with prosperity, cabbage has been a "good-luck food" for New Year's Eve, probably derived from the Pennsylvania Dutch by way of German ancestry. The southern United States took cabbage seriously but added black-eyed peas to the New Year's Eve good-luck menu.

Clover: Three- and Four-Leaf

A well-known symbol of Ireland, the shamrock or three-leaf clover is also one of the most famous good-luck symbols. According to popular belief, Saint Patrick used the shamrock to illustrate the holy trinity.

The four-leaf clover is also universally accepted as a lucky symbol. Finding a four-leaf clover brings the finder good luck. The chances of finding a four-leaf clover are estimated at one in ten thousand. The four leaves represent hope, faith, love, and luck.

The four-leaf clover was also used by Druids for spells. Clover derives its association with luck from its properties as forage or food for livestock (thus enhancing wealth and good fortune).

Grapes

In Spain, people customarily eat one grape for each of the last twelve seconds of the year for good luck in the new year. Grapes are also considered lucky for pregnancy and abundance. A plump, sweet bunch of grapes is a joyful symbol of good luck.

Hyotan (a Gourd)

The hyotan gourd originated in Africa but is an ancient good-luck symbol in Japan. Emptied and dried as a vessel, it is believed that seeds stored in it will always grow. The word *hyotan* itself is now a good-luck word. The sound of the Japanese phrase meaning a set of three hyotans is similar to the Japanese phrase that sounds like "great all-around person"; hence this phrase is good luck. A set of six hyotans sounds like "no sickness" and is also good luck in Japan.

Mushrooms

German and Austrian people believe that mushrooms are especially lucky. Mushrooms are part of the mystery of the forest. Finding a mushroom in the forest is just like finding a lucky penny. On New Year's Eve, mushrooms are often part of the decorations to bring good luck into the new year.

Pomegranates

Like grapes, pomegranates are considered lucky for wealth and fertility (lots of seeds). In Greece, it is lucky to have a pomegranate tree, and when you move into a new house, a pomegranate is broken at the threshold to bring abundance and luck.

Ti Plant

Hawaiians believe that the ti plant has the power to heal and ward off bad luck. Lucky ti leis are worn around the neck. Ti plants are also planted around homes to bring good luck. The plant was used historically for roofs, food, and medicine, which made it very useful and helpful.

Wheat

Antique butter stamps show the use of wheat as an ancient European symbol of prosperity and wealth. It was considered a good-luck symbol that brought abundance to farmers.

MINERALS

Gemstones and minerals have been held precious throughout history. Beyond decoration and jewelry, stones have been associated with properties both healing and magical. It is hard to trace just where the meaning of the stone is derived, as most of the information is passed down through oral tradition. Some sources disagree which stones are lucky and for whom they are lucky, but we offer you a general look at gems and minerals to give a feel for the subject.

In general, if something is rare or hard to get, such as gold or diamonds, it is going to be precious. A diamond, difficult to mine and requiring skill to cut, is used as a symbol of endurance because it is such a strong stone. That's why engagement rings use diamonds, a symbol of a lasting union. Gold is the color of the sun and is associated with kings and grandeur. But are diamonds and gold lucky? You might think so, but there are other, more powerful sources of luck.

Stones and Gems

Green stones typically bring good luck in prosperity and abundance.

Aventurine is found in Brazil, India, Austria, Russia, and Tanzania. A lucky stone for gamblers, it is also known for healing properties.

Jade is an Asian symbol of luck and prosperity. It has been used since prehistoric times, first for weapons and then for its royal and precious qualities. Today, it is considered a symbol of good luck. Central American societies as well as Egyptians also revered jade.

Turquoise is a blue green stone that is considered lucky to the Arabs, who called it *feyruz.* Greeks and Native Americans also held this stone in high regard. In addition, it was a powerful stone to the Aztec cultures and is considered sacred to Buddhists.

Peridot is a beautiful, clear green stone often mistaken for emerald. It dates back to the Bible. The stone has long been associated with good luck and a heart ready for love.

Birthstones

Historically, birthstones are tied to the breastplate of Aaron—a religious garment set with twelve gemstones representing the twelve tribes of Israel and the twelve months of the year.

And thou shalt make the breastplate of judgment with cunning work; after the work of the skillful workman; like the work of the ephod thou shalt make it; of gold, of blue, and purple, and scarlet, and of fine twined linen, shalt thou make it.

Foursquare it shall be double: a span shall be the length thereof, and a span the breadth thereof.

And thou shalt set in it settings of stones, four rows of stones: a row of carnelian, topaz, and smaragd shall be the first row; and the second row a carbuncle, a sapphire, and an emerald; and the third row a jacinth, an agate, and an amethyst; and the fourth row a beryl, and an onyx, and a jasper; they shall be enclosed in gold in their settings.

And the stones shall be according to the names of the children of Israel, twelve, according to their names; like the engravings on a signet, every one with his name shall they be according to the twelve tribes.

And Aaron shall bear the names of the children of Israel in the breastplate of judgment upon his heart, when he goeth in unto the holy place, for a memorial before the Lord continually.

—Exodus 28: 15–21, 29

Birthstones are gems tied to a particular month of the year and are considered lucky to people born in those months. Here are what are considered modern birthstones and corresponding months:

JANUARY	*Garnet*
FEBRUARY	*Amethyst*
MARCH	*Aquamarine*
APRIL	*Diamond*
MAY	*Emerald*
JUNE	*Pearl*
JULY	*Ruby*
AUGUST	*Peridot*
SEPTEMBER	*Sapphire*
OCTOBER	*Opal*
NOVEMBER	*Topaz*
DECEMBER	*Turquoise or tourmaline*

Note that opal is considered unlucky if it's not your birthstone.

SYMBOLS

There are many symbols that represent luck beyond those from the animal, plant, and mineral categories. For instance, the horseshoe is a widely used symbol of luck throughout the ages, as is the Italian horn. Some symbols endure as unquestioned lucky objects. Here are a few common symbols you'll come across in your quest for luck.

Horseshoe

Tradition has it that iron contained magical powers as the combination of rock and fire. Horseshoes are also crescent-shaped like the moon, which is considered powerful. Horseshoes typically have seven nails—the number 7 is considered lucky. In general, a horseshoe placed upward gathers luck and downward dispenses luck, but some cultures believe the opposite. Luck from the horseshoe is probably linked to the fact that the shoes extended the health and usefulness of the horse and therefore added to prosperity.

Italian Horn

Italians believe that the *corno* (horn) or *cornicello* (little horn) protects against the evil eye or bad luck and brings the wearer good luck. The horn predates Christianity and was originally intended to protect manhood. Its luck links to fertility, once again the ancient method of contributing to prosperity.

Chimney Sweeps

Considered lucky in the Western world, a chimney sweep brings luck to you if you shake his hand and luck to a marriage if he passes by the church during the ceremony. The luck of the sweep is no doubt due to his ability to prevent fires. It was once law in England to have a chimney swept. In the movie *Mary Poppins,* Bert the chimney sweep shakes the father's hand and his luck turns around.

Chai

The word *chai* means "life" in Hebrew and is considered lucky for that reason. The symbol for *chai* is often worn as a charm on a necklace.

Hands

Hands have been used as symbols of luck and protection throughout world culture. In ancient Rome, the upward-pointing hand protected against magic. This hand morphed into La Mano Poderosa, the Powerful Hand, used as a symbol in Roman Catholicism. Judaic and Arabic hands, Hamsa, point downward, while the helping hand of hoodoo derived from African American culture is horizontal.

Laughing Buddha

The laughing Buddha is an image, often a sculpture or a pendant, that brings luck if you rub its belly. This belief comes from the association with spiritual wholeness. Buddha's round and full stomach represents abundance and prosperity, but he gave up all of his material wealth. Buddha's luck is in the form of happiness and satisfaction rather than abundance and prosperity.

Wheel/Wheel of Fortune and Lady Luck

What the ancients revered as the wheel of the goddess is still a strong symbol of luck. The Etruscan name, Vortumna, became the Roman goddess Fortuna, with her Wheel of Fate. Fortuna is with us today but is known as Lady Luck. Her wheel is found in the popular game show *Wheel of Fortune*, the casino game roulette, and other games. The Wheel of Fortune is also a powerful card in the tarot deck and has been depicted in art for centuries.

I look to the future because that's where I'm going to spend the rest of my life.

—George Burns

Chapter 4

The Future of Luck Through Divination

It is clear that human nature compels us to look for patterns and clues to the future. The ancients progressed from their search for understanding beyond the world of symbols and into methods to predict future events. Would there be a famine coming? Illness? We are no different. We want to know if a bad flu will hit this winter and if the stock market will be higher. The Etruscans read entrails. The Greeks consulted oracles. You might read reports from the World Health Organization or track the Dow Jones Industrial Average. We want to know what will happen so that we can feel prepared for the future.

While the future is hard to predict, your personal luck within the future is another matter entirely. There might be a bad flu, but you might be lucky and not suffer from it. The stock market might go down, but not until just after you've sold your shares. Since early civilization, people have tried to find out what was going to happen before it occurred and how to either avoid problems or attract good fortune. Would there be lucky times, or would there be hardship? What will happen, and will I be lucky? These are basic questions that have been asked since the beginning of human awareness. And there have been many different ways to answer these questions dating just as long ago. Archaeologists have uncovered methods of divination dating thousands of years before Christ. Some still exist today, and many people, rational, questioning, skeptical, and intelligent people, use them.

Fortune-telling, divination, and forecasting are not exact in predicting luck but can give you insight into events and display patterns that can give you a sense of whether luck will come out on your side.

Will you be able to pick winning lottery numbers from using divination? Not likely. Most methods of divination can lend you insight into broad strokes of the future. You might have sharper insight into what is to come soon, such as if there are obstacles and challenges or smooth and easy rewards. But we still live in a world of free will that allows for some influence over future events. Nothing is set in stone. Divination gives you a glimpse that can help prepare you, but it will not reveal exactly what will happen. You can choose to use information or opt for fatalism or ignorance. You have some say in what happens, so divination is not the last word on your future. Most of these methods provide uncanny answers, though, so feel free to try them out.

The only word of caution: Methods of divination give you

some sense of outcome, but they do not say how you get there. There are always surprises because that is the joy of life and luck.

In this chapter, we will look at ancient and still-useful methods of divination. These include I Ching, astrology, and tarot, and we'll touch on palmistry and the interpretation of tea leaves. There are other methods, but we selected these for their enduring popularity and commonalities in history.

I Ching

The I Ching is associated with the Bronze Age of ancient China. It was first used only for simple divination. Will times be good? Will times be bad? Will we be lucky? In a method that was a precursor to the modern I Ching, animal bones and tortoise shells were used to divine the future and connect with the spirits. After they were burned or heated, cracks and lines would appear on the bones or shells, and these would form patterns that, in turn, held meaning. Broken lines and unbroken lines eventually became a language of prediction. Interpretations were passed down through generations by oral tradition, long before anything was ever recorded in writing. This is in part why the earliest history of the I Ching is not fully known.

In time, the patterns of lines and their related meanings were written down, and the I Ching spread in popularity. Yarrow stalks replaced bones and shells because they were easier to find. Today's I Ching methods might use sticks, I Ching coins, or even pennies.

The modern version of the I Ching is attributed to a feudal lord from AD 1150. He took the patterns of lines that had been handed down through previous generations and developed hexagrams, groups of six lines that, when created by a method of chance (like flipping a coin), can bring insight into future events, self-knowledge, and spiritual lessons.

The I Ching today is pretty much the same as it was over eight hundred years ago. It is not simple or swift to perform. You still have to throw sticks or coins (or other objects) to develop the pattern to your own hexagram, but the answers you receive are thoughtful and pertinent to the question you posed. It can be used as a moral guidebook as well as a metaphysical exploration. The language can be murky and old-fashioned (if not downright ancient), but if you find a more modern guide to the I Ching, it can be an incredibly useful tool for insight into current or future events. There are many versions of the I Ching on bookstore shelves. Some pick up on numerology or are focused on more feminine interpretations. If you are interested in trying the I Ching, chances are you're likely to find one that works for you.

Carl Jung wrote a foreword to a famous German translation (from the original Chinese) of the I Ching by his friend Richard Wilhelm. At the time, in the 1940s, Western scholars did not have a high opinion of the I Ching and thought it was only (silly) magic spells or unintelligible nonsense. It was fashionable to dismiss the entire body of history and practice rather than entertain the notion that something they didn't understand could be useful. Jung skillfully acknowledged that while the I Ching was not an easy tool to use, it suited those interested in the pursuit of self-knowledge and wisdom. The I Ching, like other methods of divination, takes time and thought—performing the tosses to get to your own hexagram will feel strange—but the information you receive through interpretation is valuable.

Regarding luck specifically, there are hexagrams and interpretations that deal directly with good fortune as well as things that stand in the way of it. The I Ching won't help you if you're standing in front of a slot machine, but it can give you insight into what might happen before you even go to a casino. The I Ching is inescapably a guide into your personal experience, so be prepared to face yourself when you read its verdict.

EXAMPLES OF HEXAGRAMS

There are sixty-four combinations of lines that form the hexagrams. Explanations of each hexagram can be hard to understand, but these broken lines and straight lines tell a story from thousands of years ago.

HEXAGRAM OF ABUNDANCE	HEXAGRAM OF OPPRESSION (EXHAUSTION)
— — — — ——— ——— — — ———	— — ——— ——— — — ——— — —

Astrology

The stars, planets, and heavenly bodies present glowing mysteries, and the earliest traces of human history reveal a fascination with the night sky. It is only natural that ancient societies studied the heavens and looked to them for guidance and information. As a part of nature, the stars were another place to search for clues to the mysteries of life and to create meaning in what otherwise seemed chaos.

In a world without telescopes, the ancients were remarkably skillful at marking the movements of the planets and recording their transits. With the naked eye, they observed the movements of Mercury, Venus, Mars, Jupiter, and Saturn and were able to predict their transits with accuracy. Through study and consideration, societies all over the world developed a way of interpreting information and made predictions that guided individuals, leaders, and countries. Astrology is considered the first science.

Up until the eighteenth century, astrology was studied as a classical body of knowledge. Even Sir Isaac Newton was schooled in astrology. While scientific study shifted toward experimentation and objectivity in the late eighteenth and nineteenth centuries, astrology has made a comeback in popularity—if not as a science, then as a tool for insight.

Astrology is credited with being the foundation of astronomy, math, medicine, and chemistry, ultimately all modern sciences.

> *Astrology is astronomy brought down to earth and applied to the affairs of men.*
>
> —Attributed to Ralph Waldo Emerson

EARLY DIVINATION BY THE STARS

It is generally accepted that astrology was born over four thousand years ago in the cradle of civilization, early Mesopotamia, near what is now Iraq. In this earliest city-state, experts called *ummanu* examined all natural phenomena to ascertain messages that spirits or gods were imparting. The skies were rich with information for interpretation—the flights of birds, formations of clouds, and, of course, the movements of the stars. From a shooting star to the simple transit of a planet, these early astrologers learned to extract forecasts. We know that they kept track of omens and predictions on cuneiforms, stone tablets etched with pictographs—a crude form of writing predating hieroglyphics. Based on weather and planetary observations, these predictions would explain the conditions that foretold of abundant crops (good luck) or disease (bad luck). Some cuneiforms can be seen in museums—but there are few reports of their accuracy.

THE BIRTH OF LADY LUCK

Myths were created to explain the heavens and the stars. The planet Venus, one that modern astrologers associate with beauty, love, fertility, and abundance, was revered by early cultures. The myth of Ishtar embodies early concepts of Venus. She held both a light, uplifting side and a dark, destructive character. Storms, plentiful crops, love, and even war fell within her domain. The interpretation of Ishtar/Venus has shifted a bit over time, but this planet still stands for love, fertility, and matters of prosperity. She is Lady Luck.

India's Lady Luck is Lakshmi. She is the Hindu equivalent to Aphrodite and Venus and is the goddess of love and beauty, prosperity, and good luck.

Japan's Lady Luck is the goddess called Benten. She is seen in many local shrines because people seek her assistance with good fortune.

Astrology flourished across the globe as civilizations developed. Chinese astrology is said to have begun around the same time by observation of the moon in relation to planets. Vedic astrology of India, documented only about five hundred years later, had certainly been an established oral tradition for hundreds of years. There followed forms of astrology in Arabic, Tibetan, Jewish, Native American, Celtic, Greek, and Nordic cultures, to name a few. Studying the stars was natural, and learning from them is a practice honed over thousands of years of existence.

MODERN ASTROLOGY

The Greeks gave us our current zodiac (which refers to the Greek word meaning "circle of animals"). The twelve signs we are most familiar with in Western astrology are based not on constellations and what they looked like (just look at the starry cluster that is meant to correspond to a sign and you'll see it's a stretch), but more likely on symbols for the seasons. Libra is the balance, and it is introduced at the autumnal equinox when day and night are of equal length. The Ram is the birth of spring, when animals mate and plants break through soil, bursting forth like the glyph for Aries, a symbol that resembles a geyser or the horns of a ram.

In early Judeo-Christian culture, astrology was in prominent use. The twelve tribes of Israel and twelve disciples of Christ also correspond to the twelve signs of the zodiac, as do the twelve knights of the Arthurian Round Table. The symbol of the zodiac is used as allegory and symbolism embedded in history.

THE BIBLE, THE STARS, THE CONTROVERSY

Most divinatory arts are controversial in terms of biblical interpretation. Astrology is mentioned in the Bible, and depending on what you read and whom you listen to, it is or isn't acceptable. The star of Bethlehem foretold of Jesus' birth. Reading the omen of that star is the use of astrology. There are many occasions in both the Old Testament and the New Testament that make reference to the stars, the heavens, and the "signs God writes upon them."

As a form of divination, astrology has a sense of history like no other. It has been used all over the world to predict the lives of leaders, the future of cities and civilizations, and it is considered the foundation of all science. Famous scientists through the ages studied astrology and were noted astrologers, including Johannes Kepler, a mathematician and court astrologer to Emperor Rudolf II of Austria who is known for his work in the fundamentals of optics. Most emperors, kings, and even popes had astrologers by their side to advise them. Until the end of the seventeenth century, astrology was a highly respected science. The growth of scientific reasoning and objective analysis diminished the use of astrology, and it faded from favor until the late nineteenth century. Still disputed as a science, astrology has roots deep in our culture and collective unconscious—and everyone gives in to reading their horoscope in a newspaper or magazine. It is simply human nature to search for information or clues to the future, whether or not it makes scientific sense.

For many, astrology provides valuable insight into basic character as well as being a helpful predictive tool.

> *Anyone can become a millionaire, but to become a billionaire, you need an astrologer.*
>
> —J. P. Morgan

THE ASTROLOGY OF LUCK

There are lucky periods in astrological terms, and it is not difficult to understand what they are and how they affect you. You'll find this explanation when you explore your personal luck profile. You won't need your own astrologer to figure out when the stars are in your favor.

Historically, there are some interesting examples of how astrology was used to help predict success or failure in the last one hundred years:

- Astrologers predicted that Adolf Hitler's campaign in Russia would fail. They were correct, but Hitler had many of them killed (he hated astrology).

- Ronald Reagan listened to astrological advice solicited by his wife, Nancy. His successful transformation from actor to governor to two-term president gives evidence that her guidance was helpful.

- Robert Zoller, a respected scholar and specialist in medieval astrology, accurately predicted the events of September 11, 2001, a year beforehand. His astrological methods are more detailed and specific than Western astrology.

- In the early nineteenth century, a poor farmer's son made a fortune in the stock market by using astrology. W. D. Gann used astrological tools to play the stock market. He is widely known for his unparalleled record, a 92 percent win rate. Gann published newsletters and left a body of work that explains his methods, although his concepts are reportedly difficult to decipher. Gann accurately predicted the stock market crash of 1929 and even wrote a novel that described the Japanese attacks on Pearl Harbor years before the event. He used both astrology and numerology (as well as other information) to reach his conclusions.

Tarot—Is Luck in the Cards?

To many, tarot cards are carnival-like fortune-telling props that are not to be taken seriously or trusted. They can be scary—the images include Death and the Hanged Man—and they might smack of deception because few people can read them well. But tarot is an excellent form of divination if you are patient and open to its messages. It is not derived from the devil, nor does it work with malevolent forces. Tarot is just another method for interpreting the events around you and showing you the choices you can make. You can use playing cards and get the same results, but a tarot card deck will bring more color and detail into a reading.

Tarot is about five hundred years old, developed sometime back in pre-Renaissance Italy, first as a card game and then as a divination device. A deck consists of seventy-eight cards, of which the first fifty-six, called the Minor Arcana, will appear familiar. There are four suits, traditionally made up of Wands, Swords, Cups, and Pentacles. These correspond to the four suits of modern playing cards, with the addition of another face card, that of a young woman. This gives each suit a King, Queen, Princess, and Prince.

TAROT SUIT	= PLAYING CARDS	= MEANING
Wands	*Clubs*	*Creativity / Passion*
Swords	*Spades*	*Ideas / Concepts*
Cups	*Hearts*	*Emotions*
Pentacles	*Diamonds*	*Abundance / Prosperity*

"Applying Tarot," in the "Personal Luck Profile" section, provides a complete list of modern meanings for each tarot card that you can use for your own luck forecasting.

In addition to the Minor Arcana, there are twenty-two Major Arcana cards that contain the more famous images of the tarot deck. These images and the words that describe them can be a little offputting, but they tell a story, just like all other divination tools. This is the story of a "soul's journey," a life cycle, not of your life, but of a situation, an idea, a phase. If the Death card comes up, it is a sign of change and transformation, not the end of a life. Each card offers an insight into the opportunities or challenges of a situation. They are not as simple to read or interpret as the Minor Arcana, but they are considered more important. The Major Arcana represent the view from thirty thousand feet above the situation. They are the big picture.

The following list provides simplified meanings of the face cards found in the Major Arcana.

TAROT CARD NUMERICAL SYMBOLS

NUMBER	TRADITIONAL TAROT NAME	MEANING
0	*Fool*	*Potential*
1	*Magician*	*Entrepreneur*
2	*Virgin*	*Intuition*
3	*Empress*	*Feminine power*
4	*Emperor*	*Masculine power*
5	*Pope*	*Hierarchy*
6	*Lovers*	*Partnership*
7	*Chariot*	*Victory*
8	*Strength*	*Strength*
9	*Hermit*	*Introspection*
10	*Wheel of Fortune*	*Fate*
11	*Justice*	*Justice*
12	*Hanged Man*	*Surrender*
13	*Death*	*Transformation*
14	*Temperance*	*Patience*

NUMBER	TRADITIONAL TAROT NAME	MEANING
15	*Devil*	*Expediency*
16	*Tower*	*Disruption*
17	*Star*	*Hope*
18	*Moon*	*Hidden elements*
19	*Sun*	*Vitality*
20	*Judgment*	*Forgiveness*
21	*The World*	*Totality*

The most obvious "luck" cards are the Emperor, Empress, Chariot, and Sun. The "unlucky" cards are typically the Hermit, the Devil, and the Tower—but this is not always the case. For instance, you could get the Tower, also known as the Tower of Destruction, before you go to the casino and get a flat tire on your trip. That's a disruption, but not a sign of bad luck in gambling. Ask specific questions, and be open to more than one answer.

Most of the other cards carry implications for your luck as well, so it is advisable to use a book or go online to get a better sense. While the images of tarot might be strong and seem threatening or dark, the messages they bear are not.

Tarot cards do not tell you how something will work out, but they do give you a good sense of what the outcome to your question will be. One of the best free online readings available can be found at Monte Farber and Amy Zerner's website, enchantedworld.com. Farber and Zerner are the authors of the Enchanted Tarot, a much more modern, comprehensive, and gentle tarot deck. A reading here will convince any skeptic of the value of tarot.

Reading Tea Leaves

Tasseography, or reading tea leaves, is considered an ancient art of divination. Drinking tea, which is a brew derived from an evergreen plant in the Camellia family, dates back so far that no one knows its origin. The first use of tea is described in Eastern mythology. One story credits an emperor from over five thousand years ago, and another attributes tea to a Buddhist monk. As long as tea has been brewed, its healthful qualities have been respected and its divination uses have been passed down.

Reading tea leaves is an art that requires a small amount of ceremony and a considerable amount of intuition. The tea drinker must use loose tea, brew it in a pot, and pour the brew into a white cup (white makes it easier to see the leaves). The tea is drunk, and the remains are swirled. The remaining leaves settle and leave an image that must be interpreted by a tea leaf reader. These images can be difficult for an untrained reader to see—you need practice and intuition.

Reading tea leaves is similar to other forms of divination in its use of symbolism. Where the I Ching interprets patterns made by lines and broken lines, tea leaf reading interprets left-over leaves from a cup of tea. Both are seemingly arbitrary patterns obtained by chance, but both give an experienced reader a great deal of insight. The same is true for throwing tarot cards by shuffling and choosing them by chance. The differences in using cards are the images, which are fixed in tarot and are not up to the reader to decipher.

Tea leaf reading can be challenging since there are many images to choose from and leaves are not picture-perfect. Common symbols include an acorn (health and good fortune), birds (good luck), a snake (a bad omen), and a toad (deceit). So many symbols are possible with tea leaves that it once again underscores the importance of using an experienced reader.

Tasseography is not only for tea. In Turkey, reading coffee grounds is an ancient art, and in other cultures wine sediment is interpreted. This is yet another example of human nature's desire to make sense of the world, to look for clues in nature.

Palmistry

Another common form of divination is found through examining your own hands. The lines of the palms, the wrinkles on your fingers and wrists, and the suppleness and shape of your hands and fingers all provide useful clues to your fortune in the art of palmistry.

Palmistry can be traced back to early India in Vedic teachings, and this form of palmistry was influential in the development of the art in the Arab world as well as in Europe. It's possible that palmistry existed even earlier than this; prehistoric cave dwellings contain detailed depictions of human hands. As with so many other tools for divination, we will never truly know how palmistry came to be.

While palmistry is associated with Gypsies and carnival fun—much like tarot—it is a tool for examining personality traits and forecasting future opportunities. Where luck is concerned, palmistry can be helpful in a number of ways.

First, dispel the myth about the lifeline. Your lifeline is not an indication of how long you will live. It is more about health and vitality—is it deep and strong, so that your life force is in full use? Or is it faint and hard to see, implying that you are not fully charged in this path? You be the judge of that.

The other two most common lines are the heart line and the head line. The heart line runs horizontally across your palm and is closest to your fingers. The head line is below the heart line, usually parallel, but there are exceptions. Your hand will indicate certain traits and abilities you possess—much like astrology—but your hand changes as you go through life. Examining the lines of life, heart, and head provide useful information about your current opportunities and challenges—your health, your intellectual mind-set, and your relationships.

Luck can be determined on your hand in many different ways, in particular by examining your fingers and the "mounts," or fleshy parts, at their base. The more pronounced the mount of each finger, the more important those traits are for you. The fingers and their mounts are associated with astrology—that's just one of the many ways in which forms of divination dovetail.

WHAT YOUR FINGERS HAVE TO SAY

Your index finger, the "pointer," is ruled by Jupiter and gives a sense of good fortune and career. A long finger indicates leadership. Short index fingers typically are followers. The mount of Jupiter (at the bottom of your finger on the palm of your hand) gives an indication of your ambitions and ability to achieve them.

Your middle finger, the longest finger of your hand, is ruled by Saturn and is an indication of challenges (and this is the finger we "flip" if we want to express anger in a crass fashion). A short middle finger indicates pettiness. The mount of Saturn below the middle finger represents sanity, sobriety, wisdom, introversion, and karmic events such as good or bad luck. Luck can be determined here by any little lines or markings.

The ring finger departs from planetary connections and is associated with Apollo. This finger represents your desire for recognition, your ability in self-expression, and your intellect. The mount of Apollo is an indication of your self-confidence and love of the spotlight.

Your pinky finger, the smallest on your hand, is ruled by the planet Mercury and represents your ability to relate to others. An elegant and long pinky finger is an indication of good fortune in communications. The mount of Mercury also informs about your ability to charm and connect with others.

LUCKY STARS ON YOUR HANDS

Look for a star anywhere on your hand, but the most important stars are on a mount. A star is a number of lines that cross one another and really give an impression of a star shape etched on your palm. If you have one, you'll see it. If you have a star on the mount of Jupiter, Mercury, or Apollo, you have good luck on your hand.

A star on Jupiter is good luck in marriage and success in life. On the mount of Apollo, a star says you have talent and can achieve fame and fortune. You might also win a lot of money.

These are only the most common signs of luck in palmistry. You can spend many hours gazing at your hand and examining the lines and markings. Being good at palmistry requires study, patience, and, as always, intuition.

Most important, your hand will alter over time. What your palm says today could change completely in a few months.

Your Future in Divination

Because we believe that there is everything to gain and nothing to lose by using the tools here, the "Personal Luck Profile" section in the book will help you examine your own future. We'll guide you through lucky stars, numbers, and other indicators that might help you attract luck and use the lucky times ahead. Because studying numbers is more complex than other forms of divination, we've devoted the next two chapters to the role of numbers and math in our understanding of luck.

This is the third time; I hope good luck lies in odd numbers. . . . There is divinity in odd numbers, either in nativity, chance, or death.

—William Shakespeare
The Merry Wives of Windsor

Chapter 5

Luck Through the Meaning of Numbers

If math and probability are the sound, reasoned use of numbers, reading meaning into a number adds a layer of subjective interpretation. Two is a quantity in math. Two is a symbol of balance, reflection, and partnership in Western numerology. Two is lucky to the Cantonese because it sounds phonetically like the word *easy*.

How and why do numbers become lucky or unlucky? What do numbers mean? Once again, human nature compels us to look for meaning, and numbers provide a playground of infinite proportion. Here we provide a broad, but by no means exhaustive, survey of how numbers are interpreted around the world. There are always numbers that are considered powerful and lucky and, of course, those that are avoided. What may surprise you is how different cultures reach those conclusions. It's not all about lucky 7.

A Brief History of Numbers

Every civilization on earth has developed a system to depict numbers. Whether it is in pictures (Egypt), hatch marks (Germany), or symbols (Phoenicia), numbers are as basic as food, language, and the observation of luck. In their simplest form, numbers quantify: For two loaves of bread, you must give me four coins. Economics and commerce began with numbers.

Not every culture counted numbers as we do, in a system of tens. Some cultures never really ventured beyond 1-2-3-4-5 because anything more was considered "many." On the other hand, as other civilizations grew more sophisticated, number systems and mathematics were born. Pythagoras is arguably the most famous ancient mathematician. You know his name from the Pythagorean theorem for a right triangle. Pythagoras established ways to study and use numbers that led to modern mathematics as well as the basis of numerology, the study of the meaning of numbers.

Numbers and Meaning

Cultures vary on what makes a number lucky.

In China and Japan, the *sound* of the word for the number is important. There is nothing like that in English, but it would be like saying "seven" sounds like "heaven" and therefore it is a lucky number.

In Western-based numerology, numbers are symbolic of quantities. These quantities in turn stand for qualities and characteristics. One has a meaning that is usually the power unity (monotheism, or one God). Two is a number of balance. Three is the number of growth, like a child born to two parents.

Gematria, a form of numerology used in the Kabala, is yet another system of assigning meaning and power to certain numbers through word values. Each Hebrew letter has a numerical value, and Hebrew words have a value of the total sum of the letters. Gematria is used to find hidden meaning in words. The Hebrew word for "loving-kindness" has a numerical value of 9. Nine is therefore a positive or lucky number. Of course, there are many ways to calculate numerical values of words and even different interpretations of numerical meaning.

Understanding the origins of some number systems helps in selecting what works for you. What is important is to become familiar with certain viewpoints of numbers and their power. It's one angle of studying what is lucky. You don't have to succumb to popular number beliefs and play lucky number 7 if you think another number makes more sense to you.

NUMBERS OF THE EAST

As we mentioned, the sound of the word in some Eastern cultures confers a quality of good luck (or bad luck) on that number.

The number 9 is lucky in Thailand. The word for 9, or *gao*, is the same as the verb for "to develop or progress." The number 9 is also auspicious because it is linked to King Rama IX. In 2003, the Thai government auctioned off the license plate 9999 for $95,200.

In Japan, the number 7 is lucky because the Japanese have

seven gods of good luck (called the Shichifukujin). The number 8 is lucky because it sounds like the word for "good fortune."

The Chinese have a long established and revered relationship with numbers that are sacred, powerful, and lucky. The number 8 is considered especially lucky in Chinese culture. The number 8, or *ba*, sounds like *fa*, the Chinese word for "wealth." In fact, the Summer Olympics in Beijing, China, are scheduled to commence on August 8, 2008, at 8:00 P.M. That's 08/08/08 at 8:00 P.M. No, that is not a coincidence. The telephone number 8888-8888 was auctioned off in Chengdu, China, for $270,723.

In contrast with the interpretation of the Bible passage in the Book of Revelation, 666 is considered a lucky number in China. The number 6 is pronounced *liu* and sounds like the word *slippery* and can also mean "everything goes smoothly." The license plate number AW6666 was auctioned off in China for $34,000.

The number 518 is also a lucky combination of numbers that means "I will prosper." Other lucky variations include 5189 ("I will prosper for a long time"), 516289 ("I will get on a long, smooth, prosperous road"), and 5918 ("I will soon prosper").

CNN recently reported that an anonymous bidder won the license plate number 12 in Hong Kong after paying $910,000 for it. The number sounds like "certainly easy" in Cantonese. That wasn't nearly as much as the $4 million reportedly paid by Albert Yeung in 1994 for the number 9, which sounds like "everlasting" in Cantonese. Additionally, the number 2 is considered lucky in Cantonese culture because it sounds like "easy."

The Chinese also developed "magic squares" that establish certain powerful combinations of numbers. The most powerful square, the *lo shu*, is said to represent universal harmony.

THE LO SHU SQUARE			
4	9	2	
3	5	7	
8	1	6	

The numbers in each row total 15. The sum of all the numbers is 45. The rows are considered powerful number combinations. Odd numbers are considered masculine and light. Even numbers are feminine and dark. This is the yang and yin, respectively. The *lo shu* square was used in the design of ancient Chinese cities and temples. It is sacred and powerful.

Gamblers look at magic squares and sometimes use their number combinations for bets. People will also be aware of number combinations popping up in everyday life, such as addresses and phone numbers.

THE MODERN STORY OF WESTERN NUMBERS

Western cultures have developed differently in assigning power and meaning to numbers. From the ancient mathematicians to modern numerologists, numbers are considered storytellers.

The Western system is derived from the Hindu-Arabic numbering system. The Hindus developed the numbering system in use today around AD 500. In AD 1202, the book *Liber Abaci*, or *The Book of the Abacus*, appeared in Italy. It was written by Leonardo Pisano, also known as Fibonacci. This brought the Hindu-Arabic numbering system to the West, replacing Roman letter-numerals and opening up vast new applications in math and numerology.

A PONY PLAYER'S VIEW OF NUMBERS

When I play horses, I use many of the numerological tools (lucky numbers, magic numbers, and Gematria). I almost always play my personal lucky numbers 512 for the trifecta. I also use Gematria and play my initials (AHD, or 1, 8, and 4) in selecting trifectas. If the odds are too long on those combinations, I look for special/magic numbers with more reasonable odds. For example, if the 1 and 6 horses are favorites, I would probably choose the 8 horse (regardless of the odds) as the third horse and play the 1, 6, and 8 for the trifecta, because 168 is a special/magic number, being the golden ratio or divine proportion (1.618). I also like to play the combination 537 because I see it often, and it is a special/magic number contained in the lo shu *square. Skill is important in picking ponies, but so is luck, and I find that numerology helps me in picking lucky numbers.*

If you consider how we count, you might recall learning number systems other than our own base ten. For instance, computer language first used a binary number system consisting of 1 and 0. In binary numbers, the only symbols to identify quantity are 1 and 0. It takes a lot of space to identify the number 8 when you can define it only by 1s and 0s; a binary 8 is written like 1000.

Our numerical system is called base ten. We have symbols that identify the numbers 1 through 9, and when we get to 10, we hit the end of the cycle and add another placeholder, what you learn in math as the "tens" place. Base ten numbers have symbols that identify quantities 1 through 9. These symbols are the numbers we write on the page: 1, 2, 3, 4, 5, 6, and so on.

Numerologists have interpreted base ten numbers as a "story" of a life cycle: 1 is the beginning, 9 is the end, and life is what happens in between. If you look at numbers as quantities, you can see how this story emerges.

One

A primordial number, the number associated with God, the energy of creation and initiation. It is the basis of monotheism.

Two

Two is polarity, yin and yang, male and female, good and evil, opposing forces that complete the whole. Two is the splitting of one's energy. Two is also balance and partnership.

Three

Three is associated with growth that brings something "good" from the split of 1 into 2. Three is associated with the holy trinity, and the number is found prominently in the Hindu, Buddhist, Muslim, and Jewish faiths.

Four

Order, stasis, and inertia are associated with 4, but this number is more about completion. There are four elements, water, air, earth, and fire; there are four directions, north, east, south, and west; and there are four seasons, spring, summer, fall, and winter.

Five

In the West, 5 is a disruptive number. It unbalances the symmetry of the number 4. Look at dice. The number 5 has an uneasy dot captive within the number 4. For this reason, Western numerology associates 5 with creativity and even love. It disrupts the status quo. It's worth noting that in ancient China, 5 was an important number, much as 3 was in the West. It stood for the five elements of earth, fire, water, wood, and metal, and you'll hear, "May fivefold luck enter!" as the door opens to the Chinese New Year.

Six

The number 6 is considered a perfect number. It is the sum of 1+2+3 as well as the product of 1×2×3. Six represents harmony and harvest. In the Bible, God created the world in six days. Six represents marriage, order, and devotion.

Seven

Seven is associated with risk and magic. God rested on the seventh day. The "seven-year itch" is based on seven-year cycles that have been observed through Saturn's transits that introduce periods of change. Seven is considered lucky in many ancient cultures, and in a few cases, the number 7 is unlucky, considered occult.

GROWTH OF 1 TO 9		
O 1 INITIATION	OO 2 POLARITY	O OO 3 GROWTH
OO OO 4 INERTIA	OO O OO 5 DISRUPTION	O OO OOO 6 HARMONY
OO OO OOO 7 RISK	OO OOO OOO 8 ACHIEVEMENT	OOO OOO OOO 9 CHANGE

Eight

A favored number in ancient times for its mathematical properties, 8 has long been regarded as the number associated with paradise. In modern numerology, 8 is the number of good fortune, money, prosperity, and achievement. It is the resolution to the risk that 7 took.

Nine

At the end of the cycle, 9 is about the last step before completion. It is three 3s, the growth of growth, the last stop of the cycle before it collapses to 1 again. Mathematical patterns of 9 add to its mystique (the sum of its multiples always reduces to 9—18, 27, 36, 45, 54, 63, 72, 81, 90, 99, 108, 117, and so on). Nine is a number that signifies change, transformation, an ending and a beginning.

Ten

Ten is the end and the beginning. Ten is 1 plus 0, or just 1. Some people interpret 10 as the end and 1 as the beginning, but it is really both. It is completion and deconstruction.

Numerology lends many tools to the study of luck. Some people believe strongly in the power of certain numbers. Others look for clues through numbers they encounter in their lives. Numerology offers insight into lucky numbers, but ultimately it is up to you to choose how to make it work for you.

In "Applying Numerology" in the "Personal Luck Profile"

section, you will have a chance to examine the many ways you can establish personal lucky numbers and what they signify.

NUMBERS IN KABALA

As we mentioned previously, Gematria is a way of looking at numbers through word values. The term *Gematria* comes from a Greek word meaning "geometry," but the most common use of Gematria is through the Hebrew, not Greek, alphabet. Every letter has a numerical value, and every word therefore is a sum of those letters. There are free websites in which you can insert a word in either Hebrew or English and ascertain the value of that word and show other words of equal value. The basic determination of letter values is different in Hebrew from what it is in Western Gematria. Here is a look at the Hebrew alphabet and letter values. Note that the name and sound of the letter is given and that they roughly track the English alphabet. Numerical values, however, are not serial as in Western numerology. After 10, they increase by tens and then by one hundreds.

Aleph—A 1	*Bet*—B 2	*Gimel*—G 3	*Dalet*—D 4	*He*—H 5
Vav—V 6	*Zayin*—A 7	*Chet*—Ch 8	*Tet*—T 9	*Yod*—Y 10

(CONTINUED)

Kaf—K/Kh 20	*Lamed*—L 30	*Mem*—M 40	*Nun*—N 50	*Samech*—S 60
Ayin (silent) 70	*Pe*—P 80	*Tzade*—Tz 90	*Qof*—Q 100	*Resh*—R 200
Shin—Sh/S 300	*Tav*—T/S 400			

Numerical values in Gematria are derived from important words. In Hebrew, God's name is "Yahweh." This is a sacred and intimate name spelled by the Hebrew letters of YHWH, or Yod-He-Vav-He, and that numerically adds up 10+5+6+5 = 26. Therefore, the number 26 is a powerful number in Gematria. Is it lucky? Kabalistic scholars have looked carefully at the words in the Bible and in the Hebrew Talmud to decipher word values that are important. They also look for hidden repetitions, or "codes," that might have some underlying meaning.

Following is the Western equivalent of Gematria, where each letter of our alphabet is equated with a numerical value. You'll note the letter values build from 1 to 26. In the "Personal Luck Profile" section (see page 178), we'll show you how to use it when looking for personal luck.

ENGLISH GEMATRIA										
A	B	C	D	E	F	G	H	I	J	K
1	2	3	4	5	6	7	8	9	10	11
L	M	N	O	P	Q	R	S	T		
12	13	14	15	16	17	18	19	20		
U	V	W	X	Y	Z					
21	22	23	24	25	26					

LA SMORFIA: NUMBERS FROM NAPLES

The use of numerical values for clues to the future and in particular luck is nowhere more defined than in Naples, Italy, with its historic system called La Smorfia (the Book of Numbers). Like *Aunt Sally's Policy Players Dream Book* from the days of the policy game, this explicit system assigns values for dream symbols. La Smorfia has defined lucky numbers for generations of Neapolitans.

La Smorfia is so ingrained in the culture of Naples that everyone knows someone who has the book of La Smorfia, the key to interpreting dreams for numbers. If a daughter of a family in Naples happens to have a significant dream and relates it to her family in the morning, La Smorfia would be consulted to ascertain the numbers that the dream was communicating, and those numbers could be played in the local lottery. Any dream can be evaluated for its numerical meaning.

Some people take their dream numbers to the local lotto every day; others wait until a dream is powerful and significant. Since there are drawings every day and as little as one euro can bring in a big payout, there is great incentive to play. All you need is a euro and a dream! The culture of La Smorfia is so entrenched that it is simply a way of life. Almost every bookstore stocks dictionary-like tomes that define the value of dream symbols. For instance, a dog is the number 4, since it has four legs. Two dogs together is 44 (as opposed to 8). If you see lips in your dream, the number is 2, but if there is a tongue showing with the lips, the tongue is 1 and the number associated would be 21. If you dream of water, here are the various meanings you might encounter:

SYMBOL	VALUE
Water in general	*51–60*
Warm water	*31–32*
Water from a sink	*23–65*
Water in a river	*67–90*
Cold water	*4–87*
Clear water	*41–86*
Rainwater	*6–18*
Stagnant water	*10–12*
Dirty water	*67–69*

As you can see from one simple dream symbol, La Smorfia is complex. Symbols and values have developed over the years and continue to evolve. A soccer star, a new politician, and even a TV show that shows up in a dream will have a number. La Smorfia is a distinctly Neapolitan source of lucky numbers, but that does not stop people around the world from using it—if you can read Italian, you can use it, too.

WHY IS 7 LUCKY?

You have probably been taught that 7 is a lucky number.

Seven is what comes up most often in dice. Seven is the time it took for God to make the world (and then rest). Seven are the ancient wonders of the world, the number of planets seen by the ancients (sun, moon, Mercury, Mars, Venus, Jupiter, and Saturn). It is a number that comes up a lot in nature, myth, and math. Seven has long been held as lucky.

Mathematicians actually have their own "lucky" numbers. They derive them by means of a "sieve," a pattern that is used to reduce integers and determine a list of these numbers. Most of these numbers are prime numbers. The list itself, of course, is infinite, but here is how it works in general.

Start with a list of numbers.

1, 2, 3, 4, 5, 6, 7, 8, 9, 10, 11, 12, 13, 14, 15, 16, and so on.

The second number is 2, so every second number is eliminated. The result is only odd numbers.

(CONTINUED)

1, 3, 5, 7, 9, 11, 13, 15, 17, 19, 21, and so on.

The number next to 1 is 3, so every third number is eliminated.

1, 3, 7, 9, 13, 15, 19, 21, 25, and so on.

The number next to 3 is 7, so every seventh number is eliminated.

1, 3, 7, 9, 13, 15, 21, 25, and so on.

After 7, the next step is eliminating every ninth number and so on. This can continue infinitely, but if you're curious, here are the mathematician's lucky numbers under 100.

1, 3, 7, 9, 13, 15, 21, 25, 31, 33, 37, 43, 49, 51, 63, 67, 69, 73, 75, 79, 87, 93, and 99.

Numbers offer infinite opportunities to try out luck. They provide messages and show patterns that can give you clues to your success. Your lucky numbers are all around you. Go figure.

Where observation is concerned, chance favors only the prepared mind.

—Louis Pasteur

Chapter 6

Probable Luck, Reasonable Luck, Mathematician's Luck

While our examination of luck has so far been concerned with history and ancient practices, it is time to look at it from a rational angle. Luck is a subject that has been studied by great mathematicians, and their work—some of it inspired so they and/or their associates would win more often in business ventures or gambling—is something we take for granted today. Great minds have considered luck from an academic and intellectual perch, and it's not hard to put their work to use.

> *Math can't predict that you will be lucky, but it's useful in predicting how lucky you need to be.*

If you enter a sweepstakes along with millions of others, your likelihood of winning (of being lucky) is much smaller than when you enter one with fewer people. You can look at odds and know how easy it is to win. Even if you know the odds of a game, you'll still be tempted to "beat the odds." Why? Because someone eventually does—but is that someone going to be you?

Probability is simply putting together a rational, formal picture of the whole: winners and losers. It just won't tell you which group you'll be in.

You need luck for that.

Mathematics and Luck

We have identified seven contributions from great mathematical minds that have helped us form a better understanding of luck. We have made their concepts simple to understand and have taken their findings a step further to help you apply them to luck. You don't have to be good at math to enjoy the results of their work.

Girolamo Cardano—a sixteenth-century gambler who figured out odds.

Blaise Pascal—a seventeenth-century philosopher who wrestled with belief and faith.

Jacob Bernoulli—a seventeenth-century mathematician who analyzed averages in the law of large numbers.

Daniel Bernoulli—an eighteenth-century mathematician who developed utility theory—the law of diminishing returns.

Abraham de Moivre—an eighteenth-century mathematician who was a consultant to gamblers and who discovered the distribution of the bell curve.

Francis Galton—a nineteenth-century statistician and explorer who established regression to the mean—how everything over time reverts to the average.

Harry Markowitz—a twentieth-century Nobel Prize–winning economist who created the concept of portfolio diversification.

Pioneer of Probability: Where Odds Were Born

Girolamo Cardano (1501–1576) was a sixteenth-century Italian physician, gambler, and mathematician.

Cardano's book *Liber de Ludo Aleae* (*Book on Games of Chance*) was published in 1525. This book contains the first principles of probability, where probability is expressed as a fraction. For example, in a simple coin toss, the likelihood of heads versus tails is expressed as 1/2. Stated another way, the probability of heads versus tails is 50 percent. Fractions make possible the concept of odds.

CARDANO AND LUCK

How can Cardano's fractions be applied to luck? In the classic coin toss example, we need *just a little more* luck than our opponent to tip the 50 percent probability in our favor. The odds of hitting the New York Lotto are 1 chance in 45,057,474.

The New York State Lottery's slogan is "Hey, You Never Know." But you do know—you know that you need *a whole lot* of luck to win a game where you have a 1 in 45,057,474 chance. Odds are especially important in pure games of chance (such as coin toss, lottery, roulette, dice, and slots) because the odds determine how much luck you need. We will have more to say about specific games of chance in chapter 7 on gambling and luck. The point here is that when you are faced with odds, it is important to ask not only the question "What are the odds?" but also "How much luck do I need?"

Cardano's odds help you decide how to evaluate "how much luck you need."

Pascal's Wager: What's Better to Believe?

Blaise Pascal (1623–1662) was a celebrated French mathematician, physicist, and philosopher.

Pascal's wager is contained in his work *Pensées* (*Thoughts*). Pascal's wager is basically as follows: God exists, or he does not exist—what should we believe? Pascal maintained that it is better to believe in God. If God exists, there is the possibility of salvation. If he does not exist, you lose nothing.

PASCAL AND LUCK

How can we apply Pascal's wager to luck? Luck exists, or luck does not exist—what should we believe? It is better to believe in luck, because if it exists, there is the possibility that we can get lucky. If it does not exist, you lose nothing. Believing in luck leads to a greater understanding of its nature, and that leads to a greater understanding of oneself.

Pascal's wager implies that believing in luck can make you luckier.

Jacob Bernoulli and Luck with Large Numbers

Jacob Bernoulli (1654–1705) was a Swiss mathematician.

Bernoulli's book *Ars Conjectandi* (*The Art of Conjecture*) was published in 1713. The book contains the theorem known as "the law of large numbers." The law of large numbers generally states that the larger the number of observations of something, the closer the sample's average will be to the true average. The law of averages describes what the true average is. In the coin toss example, the law of averages says the odds of heads versus tails are 1:1. The law of large numbers says the greater the number of coin tosses, the closer to this average you will get.

JACOB BERNOULLI AND LUCK

How can we apply the law of large numbers to luck? The gaming industry depends on the law of large numbers for profits because it can rely on its statistical house advantage over the long run. Conversely, gamblers know that if they win early, they should take profits because the law of large numbers will work to their disadvantage over time.

PRACTICAL USE OF THE LAW

The law of large numbers is useful in other luck endeavors. For example, I like to hunt for rare books. I figure on average there is one book bargain in approximately three thousand books looked at. On any given day, I am more confident of a lucky find if I look at three thousand books versus only three hundred.

Jacob Bernoulli's law of large numbers contains the idea "Quit while you're ahead."

Daniel Bernoulli and Luck with the Utility Theory

Daniel Bernoulli (1700–1782) was the nephew of Jacob Bernoulli and also a Swiss mathematician.

Bernoulli's utility theory is set forth in an essay published in the papers of the Imperial Academy of Sciences in St. Petersburg in 1738. In this essay, Bernoulli states that "the utility resulting from any small increase in wealth will be inversely proportionate to the quantity of goods previously possessed." In other words, the more we have of something, the less meaningful is an increase to it. Utility theory is also known commonly as "the law of diminishing returns."

UTILITY AND LUCK

How can we apply Daniel Bernoulli's utility theory to luck? Utility theory basically introduces a subjective component to probability theory. In terms of luck, utility theory says that it's important to make certain subjective decisions. Let's say, for example, you win $100 at a casino. Then you go on to win $1,000. According to utility theory, winning $100 on top of the $1,000 has less utility than the first $100. Anyone who has gambled knows this feeling.

Utility theory guides us out of the dilemma of whether to push our luck. Using utility theory, we should simply make a subjective determination about the utility to us of winning or losing another $100. Utility theory can also assist us in other areas where luck is involved. Let's say, for example, a collector searches antique stores for certain porcelain cups. The first lucky find makes him feel great. Now he has a thousand of these little treasures. They become increasingly hard to find. At this point, utility theory suggests that the collector should make a subjective decision and perhaps adjust his attitude to expect to find less of them and reduce his efforts toward finding them.

Daniel Bernoulli's utility theory implies that being lucky over and over again can feel less exhilarating than being lucky once in a while. It's no fun if you always win.

Luck and the Bell Curve

Abraham de Moivre (1667–1754) was a French-born mathematician. He moved to London and became a consultant to gamblers and insurance brokers on probability theory.

De Moivre's theory of normal distribution is commonly known as "the bell curve." It was first published in an article in 1734 and reprinted in his book *The Doctrine of Chances* in 1738. De Moivre describes how random drawings or events tend to distribute around their average. The distribution is known as the bell curve because it looks like a bell. The top of the bell curve represents the average and the greatest number of observations. The left side of the curve represents less than the average. The right side of the curve represents greater than average.

THE LUCKY SIDE OF THE CURVE

How can we apply de Moivre's bell curve to luck? The bell curve is a great way to visualize luck at any given time. The top of the curve represents average luck. The left side of the curve represents progressively bad luck, with the bottom being really bad luck. The right side of the curve represents progressively good luck, with the bottom being really good luck. For example, the top of the curve, in the bulk of the bell, is an average situation. If it is the average experience to win or lose $100 at a casino, that is the bulk of the curve and where most people are. The left side of the curve represents losses greater than $100, the farthest left being big losses. The right side of the curve represents winning more than $100, and the farthest right is a big win.

Applying the bell curve to luck shows how lucky it is to get lucky.

Francis Galton and Luck with Regression to the Mean

Francis Galton (1822–1911) was an anthropologist, explorer, and statistician. He created the field of study known as eugenics. Eugenics advocated improving human heredity through intervention. The scientific stature of eugenics has diminished because of Nazi abuses during World War II. Regression to the mean, however, has proved to be a powerful theory.

Galton's regression-to-the-mean theory was first presented at a Royal Institution Lecture in 1877. Galton described how sweet peas varied from generation to generation. Although there are variations, the force of nature brings things back to the average type. Regression to the mean, therefore, basically says that things tend to regress or revert back to the average.

REGRESSION AND LUCK

How can Francis Galton's regression to the mean be applied to luck? Whereas the bell curve can help us visualize luck, regression to the mean can help us with our expectations. Regression to the mean is a great way to deal with lucky cycles. If I'm having really good luck, I appreciate it because regression to the mean says eventually things will go back to normal. Conversely, if I'm having really bad luck, I can bear it because eventually things will go back to normal. You might find $20 on the street today and lose $50 tomorrow. Good luck and bad luck in this case are not equal, but Galton implies that eventually things go back to normal.

Galton will cheer up losers and challenge winners, since his regression-to-the-mean theory implies things go back to normal.

Harry Markowitz and Luck with Portfolio Diversification

Harry Markowitz (b. 1927) is an economist at the University of California at San Diego. He won the Nobel Prize in Economics in 1990.

Markowitz was studying linear programming when he published an article in 1952 entitled "Portfolio Selection." The article applied linear programming to the stock market. The central concept is that a diversified stock portfolio can be used to reduce volatility and manage risk. A diversified portfolio has stocks that are aggressive in risk, moderate, and also safe. That way, when risky stocks drop, the portfolio is buoyed by safer investments, and when risky stocks go up, the portfolio benefits as a whole.

DIVERSIFICATION AND LUCK

How can Markowitz's diversified portfolio be applied to luck? The idea is to create a diversified luck portfolio. We have previously defined luck as winning in the short term or being successful in the long term owing to chance. A diversified luck portfolio should contain both long-term and short-term luck assets. We have identified several short-term pursuits where luck is involved (for instance, gambling, book hunting, antiquing). You can create your own luck portfolio by adding to it any pursuit where you personally find luck (such as collecting, bargain shopping, playing games, participating in sports). Long-term luck may include personal relationships, career, and any other aspect of your life where you believe you are especially lucky. Sometimes one area in your luck portfolio may be "down," but another may be "up." Creating a diversified luck portfolio helps you reduce luck volatility and manage luck.

Markowitz implies that you need to take a broad look at luck. When things are going well (lucky) in one part of your life, they might be more challenging somewhere else. Lucky in cards, unlucky in love—or vice versa.

A strange sensation rose up in me, a sort of defiance of fate, a desire to challenge it, to put out my tongue at it.

—Fyodor Dostoyevsky, *The Gambler*

Chapter 7

Gambling: Sheer Games of Luck

Gambling has amused us since creation itself. Although we don't know why, we are, as humans, essentially built to bet and play with luck.

There is evidence of games of chance in the most ancient civilizations. The Iroquois played "the sacred bowl game" during the winter season. This game is seen to symbolize the life of man and the risk of reward versus failure. These Native Americans are one example of how games of chance became rituals and are simply part of the human spirit. Playing with luck is as old as man.

In this chapter, we explore gambling and luck. According to the American Gaming Association, 2005 gross gambling revenues (that is, the amount wagered minus the winnings returned to players—the equivalent of sales rather than profit) was $84.65 billion. That is over $250 for every single American.

There are two different types of gaming—games of chance (such as lotteries, slots, roulette, and craps) and games of skill (like horse racing and twenty-one). When you win at a game of chance, it's due to luck. When you win at a game of skill, it's due to a combination of skill and luck.

Even the most skilled players, however, will tell you they would rather be lucky than good.

Let's examine the major venues for gambling. These include lotteries, horse racing, and casino games. The history of each game gives a sense of how old and embedded this pastime is, and once you understand the basic rules, you can more easily comprehend the odds and what is called "the house advantage." Gambling is both entertaining and enticing—you can have fun and thrills while trying to win money.

To improve your luck, though, you need to have a grasp of what you can expect—how much luck do you need? Once you are familiar with the basic rules, the odds, and the house advantage, you have to get lucky. To help you get smart about luck, we offer eight rules of luck to help you get lucky in whatever game you choose to play. Get smart, get lucky.

Lotteries

Lotteries date back to China at the time of the Han dynasty, around 206 BC. A keno-style game was used by the government to help finance the building of the Great Wall of China. Since then, lotteries have been used virtually worldwide to finance public projects and programs. As we mentioned earlier, lotteries flourished in England and America during Colonial times and financed both personal and public projects. Today, lotteries are held in the majority of states to support education, transportation, and other public projects.

Lottery games are based on picking six, five, four, and three numbers. The odds of winning a lottery depend on the type of game played.

PICK SIX

The most popular lottery game is the pick six. In this game, the player simply selects six numbers. The odds depend on how the lottery draws the numbers, but as you'll see, the odds are daunting in any game. The amount of luck required to win is significant.

Powerball winning numbers are drawn by selecting five out of fifty-five numbers, plus one out of forty-two numbers. The odds of hitting the Powerball grand prize are 146,107,962 to 1.

The New York Lotto numbers are drawn by selecting six out of fifty-nine numbers. The odds of winning the New York Lotto are 45,057,474 to 1.

The California SuperLotto Plus winning numbers are drawn by selecting five out of forty-seven numbers, plus one MegaNumber out of twenty-seven numbers. The odds of winning the jackpot are 41,416,353 to 1.

The EuroMillions winning numbers are drawn by selecting five out of fifty numbers, plus two "lucky star" numbers out of nine numbers. The odds of winning the jackpot are 76,275,360 to 1.

PICK FIVE

Pick five lottery games typically are drawn by selecting five numbers from 1 through 39. The odds of winning a pick five jackpot are 575,757 to 1.

PICK FOUR

The winning numbers in a pick four lottery are drawn by selecting four numbers where each number is from 0 to 9. The odds of winning are 10,000 to 1.

PICK THREE

The winning numbers in a pick three lottery game are drawn by selecting three numbers where each number is from 0 to 9. The odds of winning are 1,000 to 1.

There are different ways to bet a lottery number in addition to betting a number straight, including boxing and other combinations. Detailed information on these bet types is beyond the scope of this book but can be found on the Internet at most official lottery websites.

WINNERS NEVER TAKE ALL

All lotteries keep or deduct a percentage of the money played to fund costs, projects, and programs. The typical lottery take-out is a hefty 50 percent. For example, the chances of hitting a number straight in a pick three game are 1 in 1,000. The payoff for a $1 bet is $500, not $1,000. The lottery takes out 50 percent. The payoff for a jackpot in pick five or pick six games depends on the total amount in the pool and the number of winning tickets. But lotteries will take out of the pool around 50 percent.

The chance of hitting a number straight in a pick four lottery game is 1 in 10,000. The payoff for a $1 bet is $5,000, not $10,000, as it would seem in straight math. The lottery takes out 50 percent to fund government coffers.

Lotteries have high odds and large take-outs. This combination makes it difficult to win money. The advantage is that you don't need a lot of money to play. Even if you don't win money, lotteries entertain by letting you dream.

Horse Racing

Do you like to go to the track or hope to attend the Kentucky Derby one day? You're only following the trail of ancient history. Horse racing, or "the sport of kings," dates back to the early nomadic people of Central Asia. Horse racing was part of the Greek Olympics in 638 BC and was popular in the Roman

Empire. Around the twelfth century, English horses were bred with Arabian horses brought back during the Crusades to produce Thoroughbreds. In the mid-1600s, match racing between two horses was held at Newmarket in England. Ascot was founded in 1711 and held races with several horses and a betting public. The British Jockey Club was formed in 1750. British settlers brought horse racing to America, where it was well established by the mid-1700s. The American Jockey Club was formed in 1894. Today, racetracks are found across the country. Races such as the Triple Crown and Breeders' Cup are major sporting events and are celebrated society events as well as a chance to use skill and luck to make some money.

BETTING TIPS

The odds in horse racing depend on the type of bet. You can bet a horse to come in first (win), second (place), or third (show). A *win* bet pays "2 × odds + $2." If a horse wins at ten-to-one odds and the bet is $2, you get back approximately $22.

There are also several "exotic" bets.

An *exacta* means you pick the first horse and the second horse in exact order of finish. Most tracks show the exacta probable payouts for a $2 bet rather than posting the odds. You can generally divide the probable payout by two to get the approximate odds. For example, if an exacta will pay $100, then you're looking at odds of about fifty to one.

A *trifecta* or *triple* means you pick the first three horses in exact order of finish. A *superfecta* means you pick the first four horses in exact order of finish. Most tracks don't show the probable payouts for trifectas or superfectas because there are too many possible combinations. Like lotteries, the payout depends upon the amount in the pool and the number of winning tickets. As a rule of thumb, however, you can usually multiply the odds of each horse and then multiply that number by two to get a very rough idea of the payout.

MORE WAYS TO HAVE FUN

To keep players interested and to push luck in different ways, horse racing offers other exotic bets, including the *double* (winner in two consecutive races), *pick three* (winner in three consecutive races), *pick four* (winner in four consecutive races), and *pick six* (winner in six consecutive races).

On top of this, there are different ways to bet an exotic in addition to betting it straight. These include the *box*, *key*, and *wheel.* Detailed information about these bets can be found on the Internet at most official racetrack websites.

> *There are probably more horses named Lucky than lucky horse players.*

THE TRACK'S TAKE

All racetracks take out a percentage of each dollar wagered for operating costs, purse money, and profits. The take-out depends on the track and the type of wager. Exotic wagers are usually subject to higher take-outs. Take-outs vary but are usually around 15 to 25 percent.

Horse racing offers a variety of odds. The take-out is fairly high, but it's less than lotteries. This means if you beat the odds, you get back more than you would in a lottery. Horse racing is exciting and immediate—the thrill of luck is a race to the finish.

Slot Machines

Walk into any casino (or the airport in Las Vegas) and you'll find people focused intently on feeding slot machines. Small investments, potentially large payouts, easy access, entertaining, and no skill required—it's practically irresistible.

Charles Fey became the father of the mechanical slot machine; the three-wheel game he invented in San Francisco during the late 1800s was known as the Liberty Bell and it caught on quickly. As technology progressed, so did slots. The first electronic slot was developed by Bally's Corporation in 1964. Video slots were introduced in Las Vegas in 1975 by Walt Fraley. Today, slots are fully computerized, and most use a ticket-in-ticket-out system rather than coins. Slots are cheap, easy, and seductive.

MYSTERY ODDS

Slots are different from other casino games such as roulette, craps, and twenty-one because the odds of winning on any given machine are unknown by the player. The only guidance given to the slot player is known as "the slot payout percentage." The slot payout percentage is the average percentage paid back to all players and is set by state laws and state gaming control authorities.

Casinos typically pay out more than the minimum established by the regulators, generally 92 to 96 percent. This means that the house advantage for slots is 4 to 8 percent. In other words, for every $100 wagered, the casino will keep on average between $4 and $8.

The house advantage for slots is lower than lotteries and horse racing. Many slots have tie-ins with popular television shows such as *Wheel of Fortune* and *The Price Is Right.* There are even themed slot machines that tie into nostalgic shows like *The Addams Family*, *The Beverly Hillbillies*, and *I Dream of Jeannie.* It's not hard to understand why slots are the most popular game in a casino. They are user-friendly (almost foolproof) and entertaining, and they require only modest investment—if you know your limit.

Roulette

Roulette was invented in France by Blaise Pascal in the mid-1600s. François and Louis Blanc added a single zero (0) to roulette in the mid-1800s, establishing what we now call European roulette. In America, since a double zero (00) was added to the wheel along with the single zero, double zero roulette is known as American roulette. *Roulette* in French means "little wheel." The wheel has thirty-six numbers on its perimeter.

These numbers are set in pockets against alternating red and black backgrounds (but the zero and double zero pockets are green). The wheel is spun, and a ball is thrown into it. The ball rolls along the wheel until it comes to a stop, landing in the pocket of one of the numbers, either a red or a black, or sometimes in the green.

There are a number of ways to play roulette. First, in "inside" play, you can bet one number, which is referred to as a "straight number"; for example, you put $1 on the number 22. Or you can play a combination of numbers. Inside numbers are numbers or combinations of numbers played directly—you put your money on the numbers you like. Payouts for placing inside bets are set forth in the following list. The payouts include the original bet and are based on a $1 bet.

Numbers Played	Payout
1 (straight)	*$36*
2 (split)	*$18*
3 (street)	*$12*
4 (corner)	*$9*
6 (sixline)	*$6*

Another way to play roulette is by betting on colors, odds and evens, or sections of numbers. These are called "outside" bets. Following are the payouts for placing outside bets. The payouts include the original bet and are based on a $1 bet.

OUTSIDE BETS	PAYOUT
Black/Red	*$2*
Odd/Even	*$2*
1–18	*$2*
19–36	*$2*
First 12 Numbers	*$3*
Middle 12 Numbers	*$3*
Last 12 Numbers	*$3*
Column 1 Numbers	*$3*
Column 2 Numbers	*$3*
Column 3 Numbers	*$3*

As with all gambling, there is a house advantage that must be taken into account in considering your betting. The house advantage in roulette depends on whether you are playing European or American roulette. In European roulette, there are thirty-six numbers plus a zero, or thirty-seven numbers. On inside bets, you are paid as if there were only thirty-six numbers. The house advantage is 1/37, or 2.7 percent. On outside bets, the house advantage is also 2.7 percent, because if a zero comes up, you lose your bet. In American roulette, there are thirty-six numbers plus a zero and a double zero, or thirty-eight numbers. On inside bets, you are paid as if there were only thirty-six numbers. The house advantage is 2/38, or 5.26 percent. On outside bets, the house advantage is also 5.26 percent, because if a zero or double zero comes up, you lose your bet. You need less luck to win at European roulette versus American roulette.

The house advantage in roulette is generally lower than in slots. Roulette has an additional advantage: Because the payoffs and house advantage are known, you can better manage your money.

Craps

Dice games are the most ancient form of gambling. Dicing is thought to have begun with what is known as astragali, or sheep bones. Egyptian tomb paintings dating back to 3500 BC depict games with astragali. During the Crusades, Europeans brought back dice games known as hazard, which is derived from the Arabic word for dice, *al zar.* Numerous Native American Indian tribes used dice as a form of sacred play. Today, the most popular dice game is known as craps. The modern game of craps was invented by John H. Winn in the early 1900s.

BASIC CRAPS

The most popular and basic wager in craps is called "the pass line bet," which is where the celebrated number combination 7–11 comes from. In the pass line bet, you win if a 7 or 11 is rolled on the first toss. You lose if a 2, 3, or 12 comes out on the first throw. If you roll any other number on the first toss (4, 5, 6, 8, 9, or 10), this becomes known as "the point." Once the point is established, you win if the point is rolled again before a 7. You lose, or "7 out," if a 7 is rolled before the point.

A winning pass line bet pays one to one, or even money. The "don't pass bet" is basically the opposite of the pass line bet (that is, you bet against the shooter), except if a 12 is rolled on the first roll it's a tie. The don't pass bet also pays one to one, or even money.

The house advantage for a pass line bet is 1.41 percent. The house advantage for a don't pass bet is 1.36 percent.

CRAPS ADVANTAGE

The house advantage in craps is lower than in both slots and roulette. The game may look intimidating because of the variety of possible bets, but the pass and don't pass bets offer you the lowest house advantage of any game of pure chance in the casino.

Because there are many other types of bets in craps and all have different odds and house advantages, we suggest you study the game before making these types of bets. There is a lot more to craps than 7 and 11.

Twenty-one

Twenty-one, like roulette, was introduced in seventeenth-century France and came to America after the French Revolution. In America, the game was called blackjack because a bonus was paid for a hand containing the ace of spades and a black jack—the jack of either spades or clubs.

TWENTY-ONE BASICS

Twenty-one has two types of payoff. If you get 21 with two cards, the payoff is three to two. If you beat the dealer with other than a two-card 21, the payout is one to one. If you go over 21, or "bust," you lose even if the dealer busts.

Twenty-one has a set of detailed rules known as "the basic strategy." The basic strategy tells you when to hit (add a card) or stand (don't do anything), double down (double your bet, take another card, and hold), and split (if you end up with two of the same card, you can split them and start two hands). There are many additional sources of advice and guidance for twenty-one or blackjack if you want more detailed advice regarding when each option is recommended.

The house advantage in twenty-one depends on the player's skill level and the specific casino's rules. Generally, the house advantage is thought to be under 1 percent if the player follows the basic strategy. If the basic strategy is not followed, the house advantage is significantly higher.

THE CARDS HAVE IT

The house advantage in twenty-one is lower than in slots, roulette, and craps if the basic strategy is followed. Accordingly, you should learn the basic strategy before sitting down to play twenty-one.

Luck of the Draw

Now that we have shared the basics of the most popular betting games, you can decide for yourself what you like. You don't have to bet money to enjoy the thrill of a roulette wheel or a card game. Simply playing with luck is fun. Gambling is just that—the simplest form of playing with luck and seeing how far you can take it.

Anthony's Eight Rules of Luck

Against the backdrop of gambling—casinos, racetracks, and lotteries—we offer you several rules of luck that might make your own experiences more fruitful. Understandably, luck plays a role in our lives way beyond gambling. However you might apply your play with luck—whether it is in business, love, friendships, collecting, sports, or adventure—you can use these rules as guidelines to keep you on the winning side of the curve.

Gamblers have their own preferences for games, strategies, and amounts staked. They like to gamble, but they don't gamble alike. Certain rules of luck, however, can be derived from the collective gambling experience. Here are eight rules to get lucky.

RULE 1: MAKE YOUR OWN LUCK

Make a list of the places, times, people, and things that make you lucky.

Where are you going? The place where you gamble is important. Casino gamblers often choose certain casinos because they have been luckier there based on experience. If you are lucky at a certain casino, you should start your gambling session there. The venue plays a role in other types of gambling. If you're lucky playing horses at a certain racetrack, then concentrate your efforts and money there; same for lottery tickets.

If you find lucky scratch-off tickets at a certain convenience store, buy your tickets there. If you get a bad meal at a restaurant, do you go back there? Probably not. But if you have great food and great service, you probably do return. This is luck in food. You can apply this rule of location to any part of your life.

What day and what time? Notice what days of the week you feel most lucky and also the time of day you seem to attract the most luck. Timing is a significant factor. For example, you might be particularly lucky in the early morning just as the sun is rising. You should be aware of your lucky times and play to coincide with them. There are some helpful insights into lucky times in "Applying Time," in the "Personal Luck Profile" section.

Whom are you with? The people you gamble with are also important. As a rule, you shouldn't gamble with family. As a practical matter, you don't want to compete with family while you're trying to win against the house or anything else. Family can make things a little too real—giving advice or trying to put you in your place—while you're trying to make the magic happen. You shouldn't court luck with family, with one exception—if you make identical bets or share bets so you are not in a position to compete with one another. Buy some land together, but don't bet against one another.

With friends or strangers, if you notice that good things happen in someone else's company, stick with that person. If you have a lucky dealer at a casino, play with him or her. If you stop winning when the dealer takes a break, then perhaps take breaks with that person.

What are you wearing? Clothes and props are also important in gambling. You should wear or bring whatever is lucky for you. Conversely, if certain things prove to be unlucky, you should leave them home.

RULE 2: MONEY DOESN'T BUY LUCK

Gambling is about being entertained and winning money. This rule helps you with both objectives.

Start a gambling experience by staking small amounts of money to test your luck. If you get lucky right away, you can increase the amount of your bets. If you are unlucky, then continue to play small unless and until your luck changes.

Divide any gambling experience into several sessions. For example, if you have $1,000 to gamble with, then you can have five $200 sessions or ten $100 sessions. Sessions maximize the entertainment value because you can play longer. Sessions also spread play over time, which increases the chances of playing at a lucky time.

If you are simply not winning, take a break. If you continue to play, you probably won't get any incremental entertainment value. Spending additional money won't buy you luck.

Gamblers often say that you should not play with "scared money."

This means that if you become hesitant or afraid to make a bet, you probably should not do it, because "scared money" is unlikely to win.

Dostoyevsky's main character in *The Gambler* at one point aptly says, "If you are afraid of the wolf, you shouldn't go into the forest."

RULE 3: GIVE LUCK A CHANCE

Numbers are a great way to play with luck. Games of chance like lotteries and roulette involve numbers. Gamblers often play their personal good-luck numbers. Lottery players often use birthdays or other personal numbers in buying their tickets. This is a fun way to play, because winning on a personal number heightens the entertainment value. It's also a smart way to play, because you establish some degree of fixed territory in the luck landscape.

You should also give pure luck a chance by playing a random number just in case the personal numbers aren't lucky at the time you're playing. A perfect example of this is lotteries that allow you to bet a quick pick or computer-generated number. In roulette, you might consider playing the number that came out on the last spin.

Certainly it's important to notice numbers as they come up in your life—if your gym locker is 463 and you see that number come up again in another way, perhaps a receipt for $4.63, those numbers are giving you a clue.

RULE 4: GO WITH THE FLOW OF LUCK

In theory, games of chance generate numbers randomly. In practice, patterns sometimes emerge in the distribution of numbers. Experienced gamblers look for these patterns. The disciplined gambler waits for a pattern and plays only when a pattern emerges. Once a pattern is recognized, the important thing is to go with the flow of luck. This is true in any form of risk taking. If you see the signs of luck opening up, jump in.

Going with the flow of luck implies betting that the pattern will continue as opposed to betting that it won't continue. For example, if you're playing roulette and black comes out twice in a row, you would bet that black will come out on the next spin. Obviously, there is no guarantee that the pattern will continue, but it is better to go with the flow of luck than against it.

In order to win significant money at gambling, something magical has to happen. If a magical pattern appears, you have to be there with it. Going with the flow of luck means you bet with the magic rather than against it.

RULE 5: DON'T WASTE LUCK

If you're getting lucky, it's important that you don't waste it.

Recognize when you're getting lucky. We previously described this as being on the right side of the curve. Gamblers call this being "on a roll" or "in the zone." If you're saying to yourself, "Wow!" or "This is amazing," then you should recognize you're getting lucky.

Once you recognize that you're in the zone, you should adjust your betting upward. For example, if you're playing roulette and have $1 on 17 and it hits, you win $35. You should increase the bet to at least $5. If 17 hits again, you'll win $175. If you did not increase, or "press," the bet, you would win $35.

Walking away from back-to-back 17s and not winning a significant amount of money would be wasted luck.

Even more important is to recognize when your luck has changed. It's impossible to stay in the zone forever. When you recognize that you're out of the zone, you should adjust your bets back downward. You don't want to put back the money or waste the luck you had when you were winning. It's the same in business. If you see that your strategy for success no longer works, adjust your course.

If you have won a significant amount of money, you should walk away with at least half of it. Significant means an amount of money that makes you excited or happy. Let's say winning $1,000 makes you happy. If you win $1,000 on a slot machine, then you could continue to gamble, but you should walk away with at least $500.

RULE 6: SOMEBODY'S GOT TO GET LUCKY

Right this second, as you read this, someone is really getting lucky.

In gambling (or business or any part of life), if you're not feeling lucky or being lucky, look for somebody who is. If you can find a lucky gambler, play with that person. Many types of casino games enable you to bet with a lucky player. In roulette, you can place your chips directly on top of their chips, effectively mirroring their play. In craps, you can make the same bets as the lucky shooter. In twenty-one, most casinos allow you to put money behind a lucky player's bet in such a way that if that player wins, you win. The rule can also be applied in horse racing. If somebody says that he has been hot all day, there is no harm in asking which horse he likes in the next race.

Instead of being jealous of the lucky player, play with that person. Luck can have a halo effect. This rule requires patience. You may have to wait a considerable period of time before you find a lucky player. If time is a consideration, you might not be able to take advantage of this rule. But given enough time, your patience will be rewarded if you play with someone who really is in the zone.

RULE 7: LUCK BE A LADY (OR A GENTLEMAN)

This rule is fairly straightforward—don't get angry while you're gambling. Respect luck like a lady or a gentleman. Anger prevents you from thinking clearly and rationally. It also blocks positive energy and the flow of good luck. An even temperament is often the hallmark of a good gambler. You can play with determination, but if you start to get angry, you should take a break. Luck rarely rewards a bad temper.

RULE 8: THANK YOUR LUCKY STARS

Gambling adds excitement to life. It lets us play. It connects us to the fates. It entertains us. If you enjoy gambling, then you're lucky. If you win, you're especially lucky and you should appreciate it. You can do this by sharing your luck and good fortune. Use the money wisely. Buy something, celebrate a little, bank some of it, tithe to a favorite cause, and set aside a portion for another day of gaming. A maxim from the first century BC by Publilius Syrus states, "It is more easy to get a favor from Fortune than to keep it." If you win money, remember to thank your lucky stars.

Now for good luck, cast an old shoe after me.

—John Heywood

Chapter 8

The Modern and Wacky World of Luck

It is impossible to ignore certain rituals, objects, and beliefs that individuals have found to personalize their particular connection to luck. Some of our beliefs are ancient and seemingly random. Some are extremely personal and even smelly (like old lucky socks). Here are some interesting, stimulating, and downright weird things that people believe bring luck.

Common Beliefs with Little Background

If you ask friends or associates if they believe in lucky omens, you might hear a few of these. They have old roots in cultural history, but no particular reason behind them.

You'll get money if:

A bird poops on you.
Your palms itch.

You'll have good luck if:

> *You knock on wood.*
> *You find a cricket in your house.*
> *A chicken strays into your house.*
> *Someone throws an old shoe at you before a long journey.*

Anecdotes from the Real World

There are innumerable accounts of people attributing luck to different things and wonderful, colorful stories of how luck found people in random, unpredictable situations. Here we give you some of the best stories, from our point of view, to remind you that luck can strike anyone, at any time. But best be prepared.

Sports

Of course, playing sports well and winning demand skill and talent. But every player in every sport will tell you that luck is involved as well. The most skilled athletes want luck on their side—they want to get the lucky breaks, take part in thrilling plays, and simply enjoy a winning streak. Fans want to see the best players and the big plays. Often you can't separate out the role of luck in a great play.

Here are some of the most notable anecdotes from baseball, football, hockey, and golf.

BASEBALL

Eddie Bennett

Eddie Bennett became the New York Yankees' bat boy in 1921. Between 1921 and 1932, the Yankees won seven American League pennants and four World Series.

Then Bennett was injured in a car accident in the summer of 1933, and he died in 1935. His obituary in *The New York Times* states:

> *Ballplayers are notoriously superstitious and Bennett's presence was thought to bring the club good luck. His absence during the latter part of 1933 and throughout 1934 was held by many to be the reason for the Yankees' failure to win the pennants those years. . . .*

Eddie Bennett's story doesn't end there. Warren Buffett, chairman of the board of Berkshire Hathaway, has said, "My managerial model is Eddie Bennett." He notes that Bennett's first job was bat boy for the Chicago White Sox in 1919 when they went to the World Series. He switched to the Brooklyn Dodgers in 1920 when they won the pennant. Bennett then joined the Yankees in 1921 when they won their first pennant. Buffett concludes the story with the following: "What does this have to do with management? It's simple—to be a winner, work with winners."

Lou Gehrig

One of the most memorable events in baseball history is the tribute to New York Yankees first baseman Lou Gehrig, known as "the Iron Horse," a phenomenal record-setting baseball player of the first half of the twentieth century. At his tribute on July 4, 1939, after Gehrig had been diagnosed with amyotrophic lateral sclerosis, or "Lou Gehrig's disease," he said these famous words: "Yet today, I consider myself the luckiest man on the face of the earth."

The transcript of his speech reveals that Gehrig considered himself lucky because of his fans, coaches, teammates, and family. He loved the game, and the game loved him. That's why he was lucky.

Roger Clemens

Roger "the Rocket" Clemens is one of the best pitchers in baseball. He has won seven Cy Young Awards. The future Hall of Famer certainly has skill on his side. But even the best players also want luck on their side. Whenever Clemens pitches at Yankee Stadium, he touches Babe Ruth's monument for good luck.

FOOTBALL

The Coin Toss

Football games begin with the flip of a coin. Which team gets the kickoff is the beginning of how luck plays a huge role before the clock even begins. The coin toss has been a part of professional football since its inception in 1892. Football games begin with pure luck.

The Hail Mary Pass

The "Hail Mary pass" is when a quarterback throws the football deep, hoping the receiver will catch it and score to win a game. A Hail Mary pass involves a mixture of skill and luck. One of the most memorable Hail Mary passes is Doug Flutie's forty-eight-yard touchdown pass with six seconds remaining to give Boston College the victory over Miami in the 1984 Orange Bowl. Luck and skill carried that moment into history.

The Immaculate Reception

The "Immaculate Reception" refers to Franco Harris's shoestring catch and touchdown to give the Pittsburgh Steelers a 13–7 win over the Oakland Raiders in the 1972 AFC divisional playoff game. The Immaculate Reception is a classic example of skill and luck coming together to make an exciting and memorable sports moment.

Clemson Football

Football is big at Clemson University. "Howard's Rock" is a white rock located on campus and named for the legendary Clemson football coach Frank Howard. Clemson football players rub the rock before each home game for good luck.

HOCKEY

The Stanley Cup

Professional hockey is about winning the hardware. The Western Conference champions win the Campbell Trophy. The Eastern Conference champions win the Prince of Wales Trophy. The two conference champions then compete for the Stanley Cup. Seasoned hockey fans have observed that the players won't touch the conference trophies when they are awarded. Touching the trophies may end the players' good luck while they are trying to win the coveted Stanley Cup.

Lucky Loonies

The book *A Loonie for Luck* by Roy Macgregor tells the story of the Canadian hockey teams during the 2002 Winter Olympics in Salt Lake City. It had been fifty years since a Canadian hockey team had won a gold medal. Trent Evans installed the ice for the games. He placed a Canadian $1 coin, or "loonie," under center ice for good luck. Both the men's and women's hockey teams won gold medals. The Royal Canadian Mint now issues "Lucky Loonie" coins to commemorate each Summer and Winter Olympics.

GOLF

Tiger Woods was asked in an interview what it takes for a player to win the Masters golf tournament. His answer was: "Luck. I'm not joking. You've got to have some luck. You can't afford to make mistakes down the stretch, but you've got to have some luck."

Tiger also wears a red shirt on Sundays, which is usually the final day of a tournament. Asked about the red shirt, Tiger replied that his mother said it was his power color. He went on to say, "Then wearing red became a superstition because I started playing really well on the final day of tournaments."

Gambling

Gambling brings people together like fishing—you'll hear stories of the "one that got away" or what a great hand someone played. You'll hear about the jackpot won by the guy standing next to you or the one night a woman won $75,000 playing craps. Gambling can be a lot of fun, but what keeps us all excited are those stories about the ones who really get lucky. Here are a few stories that might inspire you, too.

LOTTERY

The Story of Eight

The largest Powerball jackpot ever won is $365 million, from tickets picked by a group of eight co-workers at the ConAgra Foods Plant in Lincoln, Nebraska. The group pooled their money and bought eight five-play quick pick tickets for the February 18, 2006, Powerball drawing. They selected a lump-sum cash payout that after taxes brought them $15.5 million each.

We have previously noted that the number 8 is considered especially lucky in Chinese culture. This group consisted of eight co-workers, now referred to as "the ConAgra Eight." The ConAgra Eight bought eight tickets. The number 18 is considered lucky in the Hebrew tradition. The winning Powerball ticket was for the February 18, 2006, drawing. Whether they realized it or not, the ConAgra Eight clearly had lucky numbers working for them.

HORSE RACING

Most everyone knows Larry King as host of the talk show *Larry King Live* on CNN. Larry King is also the subject of one of our favorite horse-racing stories. Out of work in 1972, he went to Calder Racetrack in Florida with $48 in his pocket. He liked the number 11 horse, named Lady Forli. The horse was seventy to one in a twelve-horse field. He bet $10 on the horse to win. He wheeled (that is, he bet 11-All and All-11) the horse in the exacta. He had $2 left and wanted to bet the trifecta. King's birthday is November 19, so he bet 11-1-9. The race went off, and the result was 11-1-9. He collected $11,000. Let's look closer at the story. We have previously noted the value of using numerology to find special numbers. Whether he knew it or not, King used numerology to pick the winning trifecta numbers. Interestingly, the total amount that he won ($11,000) goes right back to the number of the winning horse (number 11). The Larry King horse-racing story is a perfect example of special numbers paying off.

SLOTS

International Game Technology (IGT) is the maker and distributor of prize money for MegaJackpots, which are progressive slot machines in different denominations linked to multiple casinos. According to IGT, MegaJackpots have made hundreds of millionaires and paid more than $3 billion in major jackpots. Virtually all of the world records for slot machine jackpots are held by MegaJackpots. Here's a list of the world's records for each type of slot:

TYPE OF SLOT	RECORD JACKPOT
$ .01	*$ 2,995,071.87*
$ .05	*$10,010,114.35*
$ .25	*$13,789,894.28*
$ .50	*$ 6,716,646.07*
$1.00	*$39,710,826.36*
$5.00	*$ 7,616,440.72*

The largest slot jackpot ever—over $39 million—was hit on a $1 Megabucks machine at the Excalibur Hotel & Casino in Las Vegas. The lucky winner remains anonymous.

To hit a MegaJackpot, you need to be amazingly lucky. What about winning it twice? That would win you the title of Mr. Lucky. Mr. Lucky is named Elmer Sherwin. Sherwin hit a $4.6 million Megabucks jackpot at the Mirage Hotel & Casino in Las Vegas when he was seventy-six years old. Sixteen years later, at the age of ninety-two, he hit a $21.1 million Megabucks jackpot at the Cannery Casino & Hotel in Las Vegas. Elmer Sherwin sure won. That's slots of luck.

ROULETTE

Probably the most significant story about roulette is its numerological significance. Add up all of the numbers 1 through 36. The total equals 666, also known as "the number of the beast." Anyone who has played roulette, win or lose, can tell you that it's a devil of a game.

Fyodor Dostoyevsky loved to play roulette. He wrote a novella entitled *The Gambler* that is devoted to an ardent roulette player. Reportedly, he wrote *The Gambler* in order to pay off some gambling debts. Lucky for us Dostoyevsky's passion for roulette fed his creative genius.

POKER

The most prestigious poker tournaments are the World Series of Poker (WSOP). The top prize for the winner of a recent WSOP Main Event was $12 million. Poker is a skill game. Professional poker players have to know the odds like the back of their hands. They also have to know how to read their opponents in order to tell whether they have a good hand or are bluffing. While math and people skills are integral to poker, luck plays a role as well. A popular poker expression is "I'd rather be lucky than good."

Arguably, the top three professional poker players in the world are Doyle Brunson, Johnny Chan, and Phil Hellmuth.

Doyle Brunson has won ten WSOP gold bracelets. He won consecutive WSOP Main Events in 1976 and 1977. Brunson has said, "Luck favors the backbone, not the wishbone." Brunson, however, brings luck to the table in the form of the lucky charm he calls "Casper"—a card protector with the image of a ghost on it. Brunson's lucky charm is coveted. Professional poker player Howard Lederer paid Brunson to leave Casper to him in his will.

Johnny Chan has also won ten WSOP gold bracelets. He won consecutive WSOP Main Events in 1987 and 1988. His legendary poker status landed him a role in the movie *Rounders.* Chan typically plays with a lucky orange on the table. He originally brought a ripe orange to the table to cover up the smell of cigarette smoke. The orange then became his lucky trademark.

Phil Hellmuth is the only professional poker player to win eleven WSOP gold bracelets. He won the WSOP Main Event in 1989 at the age of twenty-four. Hellmuth says that he always wears black at major championship events.

The top three poker players in the world have more than thirty WSOP gold bracelets combined, including five Main Event championships. When they sit down at a poker table, they bring both skill and luck.

Politicians and Celebrities

You can have talent and good ideas, but you still need luck to break through and become noticed. Here are some insights into luck from famous politicians and celebrities.

Several United States presidents have addressed the subject of luck.

Thomas Jefferson said, "I'm a great believer in luck, and I find the harder I work, the more I have of it." James Garfield said, "A pound of pluck is worth a ton of luck." Both of these statements relate to the interplay between hard work and good luck. It's basically up to each of us to decide the appropriate balance between the two.

Franklin Roosevelt said, "I think we consider too much the good luck of the early bird and not enough the bad luck of the early worm." This statement is significant because in looking for good luck, we also need to be aware of the potential for bad luck.

Franklin Roosevelt was superstitious. He wouldn't sit at a table with thirteen guests. By contrast, Woodrow Wilson believed that 13 was his lucky number.

Harry Truman loved to play poker. Truman said, "Luck always seems to be with me in games of chance and in politics."

GOOD LUCK GONE BAD

In World War I, Adolf Hitler was a young soldier in the Bavarian regiment. He became known for his good luck in escaping injury during dangerous missions—2,500 of 3,000 men in his regiment were killed, and he remained untouched. He ended up using the good-luck swastika and turning its good fortune into a force of evil.

CELEBRITY LUCK

Talent is necessary. An opportunity is crucial. Being well-known in the field you choose requires both—and lots of luck.

Edward R. Murrow was a legendary broadcast journalist for CBS. His famous sign-off line was "Good night, and good luck." He began using the phrase to close his reports during World War II and continued using it through the 1950s. The words *good luck* become especially poignant during wartime or times of national crisis.

In an interview about the film *Match Point*, Woody Allen said, "I wrote the film because I wanted to write about the effect of luck in our lives. Humans are so dependent on luck and so afraid to admit it, because it means a lot of things are out of our control and we don't want to think that." Allen implies that we shouldn't be afraid to explore luck and the role it plays in our lives. In many ways, luck is our personal frontier. The extent to which we explore it is for each of us to decide.

An important piece of luck from the theater is the song "Luck Be a Lady," written by Frank Loesser for the Tony Award–winning musical *Guys and Dolls.* Frank Sinatra's rendition of "Luck Be a Lady" is probably playing at some casino right now. The song is filled with hope and energy, and hearing it reminds us how lucky we are to have luck in our lives.

Ivy League Luck

The best and the brightest students attend Ivy League schools. They know they need to be smart and that they need luck on their side. Here is just a glance at the good-luck rituals these students perform.

At Yale University, students rub the toe of the statue of Theodore Woolsey for good luck.

At Harvard University, students rub the toe of the statue of John Harvard.

At Brown, students rub the nose of the bust of John Hay.

At Dartmouth, students rub the nose of the bust of Craven Laycock and Warner Bentley.

These students have to prove how smart and achieving they are just to get into Ivy League schools. They still court luck. You should be doing the same.

Part Two

Personal Luck Profile

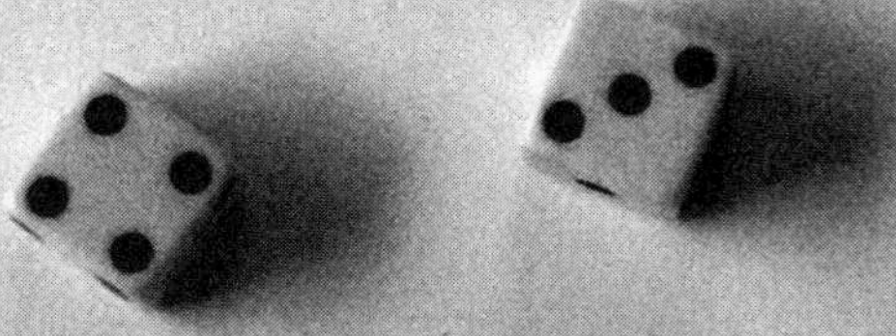

What we call luck is the inner man externalized. We make things happen to us.

—Robertson Davies

Luck has been heavily explored and analyzed throughout history. Although you won't see separate teachings of the subject, you can see how luck stands firmly at the center of man's attempts to understand the world.

As we've seen, the environment gave luck's first clues. Through the study and observation of planetary movements, numbers, cards, time, herbs, colors, stones, and charms, civilizations formed opinions and beliefs about what would attract good fortune and how to predict times of good luck. Luck has been studied seriously, flirted with coyly, and minimized with skepticism. But it's still here, attracting our attention and daring us to catch a glimpse.

You can actually learn from your ancestors now. You might not think that people who lived so long ago could have anything substantial to teach. But the earliest sciences based on stars and symbols somehow managed to work well in predicting future events. We will share with you information that has been time-tested and accurate in forecasting. You're the one who has to determine whether to use it.

In this section, we'll help you track your personal connection to luck and give you a basic understanding of how you can apply this knowledge and experience to your life. It's not enough just to know what numbers mean or that you're a Capricorn. You can take stock of your personal numbers, personal planets, and personal cycles and begin to predict lucky phases in your life. You'll begin to read and use color, even flowers and herbs, to bring extra magnetism to your lucky powers. And symbols that might have once been dismissed as meaningless will bring you deeper understanding of how you've been working with luck all along.

Trace personal luck patterns with these tools:

1. Astrology
2. Numerology
3. Tarot
4. Time
5. Herbs
6. Colors
7. Stones
8. Charms

Will this work? Hindsight is always the best way to know. In our experience and practice, we can see results. Moreover, once you embed these ideas into your life, you'll more easily practice the art of working within the currents of luck. You won't be successful if you try too hard. Once you're done thinking about the nature of luck, it will sink back into your second nature wiser and more secure.

Before You Get Started

Here are some instructions to keep in mind before you embark on your journey to personal luck.

- Each section provides you with the basic building blocks of your personal luck profile.
- Keep track of each planetary placement and each number of significance so that you can put together your personal luck profile.
- Use the Personal Luck Profile Worksheet provided on page 201.

LOOK FOR PATTERNS

Before you set out to trace your steps on the path to personal luck, get into the right mind-set. What you'll be looking for are patterns, where planetary cycles and numerological cycles come together. Here you will see a profound pattern of ups and even downs in your life.

LOOK BACKWARD FIRST

With this information, look back into your life where you experienced great waves of fortunate events. Perhaps you got your first great job, or you were promoted. Maybe you won a lot of money at a casino or you ran in a marathon. Everything you consider good counts—love, money, property, and health—it's all about good times. See where the planets were and what your key numbers were at that point in your life. You're bound to see convergences and patterns.

Of course, you can do the same with more difficult phases that you've encountered and see patterns where luck was less powerful.

LOOK AHEAD SECOND

Once you get a feel for your prior cycles with planets and numbers, you can project good years and periods of time ahead of you. With this information, you know you'll have luck on your side if you want to take risks or strive for more in your life. Conversely, when you see patterns that are clearly not favorable, step aside and let the status quo be your luck.

If you need a reminder of your astrological sun sign, find where your birthday falls in the following chart. That is your sun sign.

SUN SIGNS	
ARIES	*March 21–April 20*
TAURUS	*April 21–May 21*
GEMINI	*May 22–June 21*
CANCER	*June 22–July 22*
LEO	*July 23–August 21*
VIRGO	*August 22–September 23*
LIBRA	*September 24–October 23*
SCORPIO	*October 24–November 22*
SAGITTARIUS	*November 23–December 22*
CAPRICORN	*December 23–January 20*
AQUARIUS	*January 21–February 19*
PISCES	*February 20–March 20*

Applying Astrological Luck

As you now know, astrology was considered one of the first sciences in the history of man. Astronomy regarded only the planetary positions, but astrology gave these positions meaning. From earliest man, planets and signs were read with incredible detail. A great deal of faith was put into reading the stars—cities as old as Baghdad were established based on the stars, and rulers were appointed at birth when their charts showed greatness for leadership. It was truly considered a science to live by. Scholars vied for apprenticeships with astrologers of great repute. It might surprise you to know that up until about two hundred years ago, astrology was still considered so important that even popes retained their counsel. Kings, warriors, and diplomats all over the world relied (and still do!) on information from the stars for wisdom and success. The Reagans, much maligned for consulting astrologers during the presidency, really had the last laugh. As a two-term president who escaped serious harm from a would-be assassin and achieved a fairly scandal-free tenure, Ronald Reagan was certainly born with lucky stars, and he used them wisely.

Astrology can be useful in trying to understand when you will be personally lucky. It's fairly easy to examine stretches of opportunity—the times when luck is more likely to play in your favor. It's also easy to figure out when the tide will turn. But while astrology can pinpoint influences over months and years, it won't tell you what day to play the Powerball or when you'll get a windfall. Using astrology gives you the broad strokes of luck's path, and it's entirely worth using—and it's just one of several tools that will give you a handle on your personal luck.

In Chinese astrology, each person is allotted a share of good fortune at birth. When you're out, you're out.

How the Stars Work for You

Astrology holds two main planets responsible for luck: Venus and Jupiter. Saturn is the planet that causes hardship and delays, and it is generally not lucky to take risks or expect things to sort out favorably with certain aspects of this planet. Once you get familiar with these heavenly bodies, you can track how they flow through your life.

PLANETS OF LUCK AND CHALLENGE

***Venus**—love, money, beauty—a lucky planet that moves quickly through the zodiac, making it to every sign almost every year.*

***Jupiter**—the planet that rules luck itself, risk taking, resilience, and expansion. It takes twelve years to go through the whole zodiac, so when it's in your sign, it stays there for a whole year.*

***Saturn**—perhaps unfairly known as the "killjoy" planet. Saturn tempers both Venus and Jupiter influences, making it harder to fall into luck. In any showdown between planets, Saturn always wins. It takes about twenty-nine years to ride through the entire zodiac, so it takes a little over two years to go through each sign.*

VENUS

Venus is well known for its influence on love, money, and beauty—it rules all three in astrology. Yet Venus also gives you some indication of how comfortable you are in the pursuit of luck and risk taking as well as what makes you happy. Venus contributes to your personal attitude toward luck, and understanding it will help you connect to the things that make you lucky.

JUPITER

Jupiter is the planet that rules higher thinking, expansiveness, adventure, and risk. It can be an indication of your core values as well as a clue to where your most optimistic energies may be.

HOW TO FIND YOUR VENUS AND JUPITER

When Jupiter or Venus (or both) transit advantageous points in your stars, you could be going through a lucky phase. Find your birthday in the Venus and Jupiter charts in appendixes A and B. Go to the year you were born and the closest month and day listed that is prior to your birthday. That will tell you which sign of the twelve zodiac signs Venus or Jupiter is in for you. Then read the corresponding descriptions provided here to see what Venus and Jupiter mean for you.

VENUS IN YOUR LIFE

Venus flies through the entire zodiac rather swiftly, often making it through all twelve signs in a year. Venus also travels close to the sun, never more than two signs away (sixty degrees) from your sun sign.

Venus is generally a planet that brings pleasure and happiness. Venus charms your life in a certain way, depending on what sign it's in. With Venus in a helping position in your chart, your chances for good luck or achieving the right outcome are improved. However, Venus has negative traits as well. Too much of a good thing is sometimes attributed to Venus's drive for pleasure. Too much drink, food, sex, and even gambling can all be too much Venus. As you explore where Venus lives in your chart, you'll pay attention to when you're more likely to enjoy maximum pleasure or seek to minimize unpleasant realities. If you're especially interested in being lucky in love, Venus is your planet.

Venus in Aries

You are independent, enthusiastic, and game for anything. Having Venus in Aries makes you able to go for what you want. Downside? Going too hard and fast without looking around to see where you are. You are lucky when Venus is in Aries, but it could make you too quick off the draw.

Good-luck phases: Venus in Aries, Leo, and Sagittarius.

Venus in Taurus

Venus is at home in the sign of Taurus, happy to loll in luxury and comfort. Venus is lucky with property, real estate, jewels, and money. Having Venus in Taurus is good luck for making money, but also rather good at spending it. You could be penny wise and pound foolish. Venus in Taurus is lucky with investments that are either in things you love (like art and antiques) or in securities that have conservative staying power.

Good-luck phases: Venus in Taurus, Virgo, and Capricorn.

Venus in Gemini

You are smart, fun, and a great salesperson. Venus in Gemini brings luck in words and wisdom. Of course, social contacts can bring great luck in getting jobs or getting in on a deal. Your attention span, however, can challenge your ability to follow through. Venus in Gemini is most lucky when you can balance fun with real work effort and put up with the tedium of due diligence. Otherwise you'll be full of stories about how you could have/should have but didn't.

Good-luck phases: Venus in Gemini, Libra, and Aquarius.

Venus in Cancer

You're a home-loving person with loyalty to family, and your luck comes through close associations. You aren't especially trusting, so you aren't likely to be taken advantage of. In fact, you're a bit risk-averse, so that even when you're feeling lucky you might not act on it. The most effective luck will happen when it involves people you love—your family and friends.

Good-luck phases: Venus in Cancer, Scorpio, and Pisces.

Venus in Leo

You're a winning light. Venus in Leo loves to lead a charge. You're also someone a lot of people believe in, and you'll draw a lot of positive support from people you don't even know. You are born with lucky resilience and optimism. You can use your luck in any area you like. Just don't push it too much—Venus in Leo serves no master.

Good-luck phases: Venus in Leo, Sagittarius, and Aries.

Venus in Virgo

No one puts one over on you. Venus in Virgo is lucky in smarts. You can spot a rotten apple and a phony baloney a mile away. Your natural sensors guide you away from trouble and into places of success. Your only caution is not to tell everyone else. You like to instruct, and sometimes you lose out because you've shared too much.

Good-luck phases: Venus in Virgo, Capricorn, and Taurus.

Venus in Libra

Venus is at home in two signs, Taurus and Libra. In the air sign of Libra, Venus brings beauty, charm, and intelligence. You could be someone else's good-luck charm because of your natural magnetism. Your luck is usually in love, but you can also be lucky in persuading people to do your bidding. Great lawyers and generals often have Venus in Libra.

Good-luck phases: Venus in Libra, Aquarius, and Gemini.

Venus in Scorpio

This is an intense placement of Venus, and luck is a huge part of life. Venus in Scorpio brings more than 100 percent commitment to any endeavor, especially if pleasure is involved. You could have luck in gaining money through marriage, death, or legacy. And you could have a great time spending every cent.

Good-luck phases: Venus in Scorpio, Pisces, and Cancer.

Venus in Sagittarius

Fun-loving and adventure-seeking, this sign endows Venus with a sense of risk and bounce. With Venus in Sagittarius, you're lucky in the businesses of travel or shipping. This is also the one placement of Venus that suggests (not *promises*) luck in speculation and investment. The great thing about Venus here is that even if you fall, you get right up again. Optimism and the need for levity usually win out.

Good-luck phases: Venus in Sagittarius, Aries, and Leo.

Venus in Capricorn

Venus takes a turn for more serious matters in Capricorn and gives you a desire for respect and rank. Venus in Capricorn typically brings luck in business with promotions and people who like to do you favors. You might prefer to achieve and acquire more than you like to enjoy, though. Venus here needs status, but not without warmth. Remember to listen to your heart to add to your luck.

Good-luck phases: Venus in Capricorn, Taurus, and Virgo.

Venus in Aquarius

In the airy and unpredictable sign of Aquarius, Venus is a bit spontaneous. Fast friendships and romances can form with ease. Venus here attracts lucky friendships and situations that quite unpredictably lead to good fortune. Follow your intuition and you'll be where you want—and have what you want.

Good-luck phases: Venus in Aquarius, Gemini, and Libra.

Venus in Pisces

Venus is in a happy place in Pisces. If it's beautiful, Venus in Pisces will find it and love it. Your nature is to find harmony, peace, and hope, and in doing so, you attract good luck through people. If you are sour, though, you're likely to suffer more than others. Lean into the light and you find life is good.

Good-luck phases: Venus in Pisces, Cancer, and Scorpio.

JUPITER IN YOUR LIFE

The planet most associated with luck and its beneficial properties is Jupiter. If you were born with Jupiter in the sign of Sagittarius or if your sun sign is Sagittarius, you are already born with a little luck. When is that luck active? That's what we're about to tell you. Even if you don't have Jupiter in Sagittarius, you will have lucky phases and the benefits of Jupiter's energy.

Among Jupiter's gifts are self-confidence, risk taking, hunches, and resilience. It is also the planet that encourages exploration and the pursuit of knowledge. Foreign affairs, cultural exchange, advanced studies, and philosophy are this planet's domain. Jupiter's expansive energy is what helps individuals take risks to improve lifestyle. Jupiter typically influences job promotions, new homes, new babies, and new opportunities in most areas of life. When Jupiter is transiting your own sign, its expansive energy can also enlarge your waist size, so not all of Jupiter's effects are necessarily positive.

In matters of luck, however, you want Jupiter on your team. Jupiter's revolution around the sun takes about twelve years. When you were born, Jupiter was in one of the signs of the zodiac, and every twelve years it returns to that sign. Cycles of luck under Jupiter are every twelve years.

When Jupiter enters your sun sign, you'll also experience a boost of good luck. Most people will have two twelve-year cycles, one when Jupiter returns to the place it was when you were born and the other when Jupiter enters the sign of your sun. Some, of course, will find that Jupiter is in the same sign as their sun. Those twelve-year cycles will be even more important.

JUPITER IN THE SIGNS

Each sign responds to Jupiter's influence differently. Here is a digest of what to expect with your own Jupiter placement. Again, check the tables in appendix B to find the year you were born and the closest month and day listed that is prior to your birthday. That will tell you which sign of the twelve zodiac signs that Jupiter is in for you. Then read the corresponding description provided below to see what Jupiter means for you.

Jupiter in Aries

The exuberant and adventure-thirsty sign of Aries is a great place for Jupiter. You're fearless. Risk taking is almost like eat-ing candy—it's really good while it's going down, but when it's over you might regret how much you had. You're up for anything as long as it's interesting and challenging—something new is always better than "been there, done that." If you can find a way to focus your risk taking and to listen to the cautions of others who might be more grounded, you'll find that success and luck are with you more often than not. You could push your luck by not noticing when it turns. You could get carried away by competition or distracted if you have too many goals in mind—the danger is to spread your risks too thinly.

Jupiter in Taurus

In the grounded sign of Taurus, Jupiter brings luck to practical and down-to-earth pursuits. You are someone who will do well in banking, real estate, and luxury items. You aren't, however, interested in the thrill of risk. You are more likely to enjoy a straightforward plan to achieve what you want, and your investment instincts are good. If you get too carried away with making money for money's sake, however, you won't be as happy as you think you should be. Luck comes in the material world only because you enjoy it. Acquisition isn't a good enough reason to exist. Enjoyment is. If you find that you're hoarding or pack-ratting away your winnings, your luck will be meaningless. You can't take it with you, right?

Jupiter in Gemini

The characteristics of Jupiter in the lively communications sign are intellectual and energetic. Jupiter expands the mind in Gemini, bringing innate wisdom as well as the thirst for learning more. In the realm of the mind, Jupiter generates many new concepts and inventions. Alexander Graham Bell, for instance, had Jupiter in Gemini—as the inventor of the telephone, he couldn't have done more for the field of communications in his lifetime. Your Jupiter will also make you naturally charming and entertaining; these qualities bring luck with people to the forefront. But you might also be living in your head, where inventiveness and breakthrough ideas can be found. As long as you don't devote too much time to overthinking or second-guessing, you will be able to harness the luck that comes with such smarts.

Jupiter in Cancer

The home-loving sign of Cancer at first might seem to be an odd place for the planet that loves to roam, but it is a fortunate placement for luck. Jupiter in Cancer is extremely intuitive. While you will desire a private life and certainly a steady and happy home, you are gifted in connecting with others on a large scale. Your luck is in your ability to feel out the future and help shape it. Individuals with Jupiter in Cancer include great philanthropists, ballplayers (Babe Ruth!), and musicians. You are endowed with a strong, steady talent to connect with others, but you also know how to keep your life your own. When Jupiter transits are fortunate, you will thrive; and when they are not, you will still be happy.

Jupiter in Leo

Fire signs love Jupiter, and Leo is no exception. The sign of Leo represents leadership, pride, and all pleasurable pursuits.

Jupiter is a people magnet—it draws in those who would like to be led. It's also a blame deflector—Jupiter in Leo manages to get away with a warning when others could get jail time. But it's not always easy street. Leo likes gaming, and Jupiter is easily carried away. Don't look to others to tell you when you've had enough, because it is very likely that you surround yourself with "yes" people. Instead, find a way to set your own limits and know when you hit them. Jupiter in Leo is lucky, but it's not foolproof.

Jupiter in Virgo

In the careful and slick-smart sign of Virgo, Jupiter is relegated to more practical matters. Health is good—and you'll have to agree that this is your more precious asset. Your mind is crazy brilliant, also a helpful trait. But you can also overthink, over-analyze, and find minutiae fascinating. You're not a big risk taker unless you've done your homework and believe the risk is truly worth it. You're also one to respect good fortune when it comes and understand that it's not going to last forever. If there's anything you don't do enough of, it's relaxing and enjoying yourself. Enjoy good luck when you have it, and stop worrying about times when you don't—you're smart enough to survive either way.

Jupiter in Libra

Expansive Jupiter in the air sign of Libra makes a very smart strategist. It's not likely that you'll ever really need luck to solve a problem or to get what you want because of your brilliant mind. Luck, of course, will play a part in the way opportunities come to you and if you're paying attention. But on the whole, you're smart enough to play out any hand. Even in a bluff, you could win. What will make you most uncomfortable is someone just as smart as you are. Conflicting opinions or well-armed competitors could cause you to shy away from what you want. If luck is on your side, don't give up. But if luck isn't there, see ya.

Jupiter in Scorpio

You are as lucky as you want to be. Jupiter's energy in Scorpio is intense, focused, and hard to control. So you can be intentionally dark, down and out, or strong, up, and can-do. You can't always choose what direction you'll go in, but one thing is for sure: When you're up, you're a winner. Your charm, wit, and uncanny intuition are unparalleled in any situation when luck is with you. You'll even get farther than you think you can. Even when you're lucky, though, you could temper your abilities by worrying about the time when your luck runs its course. Balancing optimism and practicality takes practice—don't stop trying.

Jupiter in Sagittarius

Here is the luckiest placement of the luck planet in the entire zodiac. Jupiter is at home in Sagittarius, so it is the strongest influence it can be. You are brave, resilient, adventurous, and basically lucky. This isn't to say you'll never have a day of bad luck or unhappiness. Jupiter in Sagittarius only means that you'll be guaranteed some good times ahead. You have luck cycles like everyone else, and when Jupiter returns to Sagittarius every twelve years, it signals a reignition of luck, power, and excitement. Don't neglect problems, though. They'll expand until you solve them.

Jupiter in Capricorn

Tempered by the cautious energy of Capricorn, Jupiter here is lucky in traditional and practical pursuits. This isn't a happy-go-lucky risk mentality. Instead, your luck is in steady progress, smart, authoritative action, and patience. Business and commercial enterprises that require structure are great playgrounds for you. Rules can be bent, but you're best not testing limits too broadly. In adverse conditions, you're more likely to restrict your risks almost too much. Find a balance in both optimistic and challenging times, and your luck will hold.

Jupiter in Aquarius

This placement of Jupiter has humanitarian and leadership qualities. Your luck leads you in a general sort of way. As a very inventive and forward-thinking individual, you're not terribly aware of exactly what's happening right in front of you. You're too busy reaching into the future and shaping events to your liking. You typically feel lucky because you see hope and opportunity in the future. Of course, you're still able to enjoy lucky cycles, but you won't feel "off" years as acutely. In general, while abundance and prosperity are agreeable, Jupiter in Aquarius makes you feel lucky and happy in more powerful ways, through peace of mind and faith.

Jupiter in Pisces

With lucky Jupiter in the bliss-loving sign of Pisces, you know a good thing when you see it. Your heart is huge, your love is boundless, and your ability to find joy makes for great adventure. You love helping others. You love music, poetry, and art. You love animals and nature and pretty much anything and anyone of beauty. Jupiter puts you in luck's way through friends and acquaintances that could give you opportunities for money, position, and a good life. You, however, have to make time to work so you don't blow the chances you're given. You could find pleasure almost anywhere, but you have to allow for the hard work of life, too.

> *Good luck comes from Jupiter in two ways: when it enters your sun sign and when it enters the sign it was in when you were born.*

SATURN: CHALLENGING LUCK

Ancient astrologers always looked at Saturn's placement to know where adversity and challenge might be found in the chart of a ruler, city, or country. Modern astrologers are no different. There is no point in examining only the positive influences of planets, because you won't get a realistic picture of luck's power.

Saturn is known as a tempering influence. In its most difficult positions, it challenges and opposes you so that you don't get what you want—at least not right away. Saturn is a powerful planet that actually represents karmic work. You need to face Saturn's tests so that you can progress through your life with some learning and accomplishment. Saturn isn't bad luck, but it makes you appreciate good luck when it's on your side.

Saturn transits take even longer than Jupiter's revolutions. Saturn will voyage through the entire zodiac in a little over twenty-eight years.

You will feel those Saturn transits most acutely at ages fourteen to fifteen, twenty-eight to thirty, forty-two to forty-five, and fifty-seven to sixty. In those cycles, Saturn is in opposition to or conjunction with the place it was in your birth chart. Saturn is also powerful when it opposes the sign of your sun.

Although Saturn in your own sign can be tough, it is usually lucky at the end of its transit. To make the most of your astrological luck analysis, you must line up Saturn with all the other planetary transits you've identified.

> *True luck consists not in holding the best cards at the table: Luckiest he who knows just when to rise and go home.*
>
> —John Milton Hay

No matter how favorable Jupiter and Venus might be, Saturn always wins. If you find that Jupiter and Venus converge in your sign while Saturn is also there, you'll have good luck after working very hard to earn luck's rewards.

To give you a brief idea of Saturn's influence in your birth chart, look in appendix C and find the year you were born and the closest month and day listed that is prior to your birthday. That will tell you which of the twelve zodiac signs Saturn is in for you. Following are the corresponding descriptions of the general challenges facing everyone who has Saturn in that sign.

Saturn in Aries

Determined, ambitious, and smart, Saturn in Aries is great for an independent operation. When you need to be soft, vulnerable, and forgiving, however, you're in for a bit of a challenge. Watch your ability to be in a partnership.

Saturn in Taurus

You are naturally compassionate, but you can be stubborn to the point where it doesn't make sense. Saturn wants you to work hard on home and possessions.

Saturn in Gemini

Saturn gives you a penetrating, gifted mind and perseverance to accomplish what you want. You are not likely to be lucky with relatives or legalities, though.

Saturn in Cancer

Saturn gives you strong psychic talents and positive influence around others. But Saturn here can make you moody and dissatisfied with home life.

Saturn in Leo

You're a strong leader, but you can't always trust those you lead. Saturn in Leo can bring challenges to love and children.

Saturn in Virgo

You're very intelligent, but your tendency to overanalyze can make you unsure and self-doubting. When you're challenged, you could have problems with employment or self-confidence.

Saturn in Libra

Saturn in Libra is strong and gives you deep intelligence. Marriage might be delayed, and problems with women are associated with Saturn in this sign.

Saturn in Scorpio

Too clever for your own good, Saturn in Scorpio makes you so smart that you can outwit a lot of people to get what you want. Unfortunately, you can pay the price for being secretive.

Saturn in Sagittarius

You're gifted with an astute mind and the ability to improve yourself and others. Saturn here also holds grudges, though, and those can keep you from getting ahead.

Saturn in Capricorn

At home in this sign, Saturn in Capricorn brings cautious ambition and the tactics you need to accomplish what you want. Friends may not be reliable, however, and you'll worry too much, which taints the taste of success.

Saturn in Aquarius

Saturn here gives you a great and respected legacy through your ideas and discoveries. In general, you'll end life better than you started. Challenges are in friendships.

Saturn in Pisces

Saturn in Pisces gives you an amazing understanding of the world as well as strong psychic qualities. If you can maintain a positive attitude, you can avoid being overwhelmed by it all.

Saturn's Punches

When Saturn is opposite your sun sign, you'll find it most difficult to access good luck. When Saturn is in your sun sign or at a ninety-degree angle (it's called a "square" in astrology), you'll find that luck isn't beyond your reach, but you'll have more challenges and delays than you like.

SATURN'S EFFECT ON LUCK		
YOUR SUN SIGN	LUCK IS MOST CHALLENGED IF SATURN IS IN	LUCK IS SOMEWHAT CHALLENGED IF SATURN IS IN
Aries	*Libra*	*Aries, Cancer, Capricorn*
Taurus	*Scorpio*	*Taurus, Leo, Aquarius*
Gemini	*Sagittarius*	*Gemini, Virgo, Pisces*
Cancer	*Capricorn*	*Cancer, Libra, Aries*
Leo	*Aquarius*	*Leo, Aquarius, Taurus*
Virgo	*Pisces*	*Virgo, Gemini, Sagittarius*
Libra	*Aries*	*Libra, Cancer, Capricorn*
Scorpio	*Taurus*	*Scorpio, Aquarius, Leo*
Sagittarius	*Gemini*	*Sagittarius, Virgo, Pisces*
Capricorn	*Cancer*	*Capricorn, Libra, Aries*
Aquarius	*Leo*	*Aquarius, Taurus, Scorpio*
Pisces	*Virgo*	*Pisces, Gemini, Sagittarius*

Finding Your Lucky Periods in the Future

To find lucky periods of time for a given year in the future, follow these steps:

1. Venus periods.

Find the year you want to examine in appendix A. Find the three signs that Venus is lucky for you based on the description provided earlier, and determine the corresponding dates. Those are your lucky Venus periods.

2. Jupiter periods.

Go to the same year you want to examine in appendix B and look to see what sign Jupiter is in for that year or closest prior year. If it is your sun sign or in the sign that Jupiter was in when you were born, this is an especially lucky period.

3. Saturn periods.

In that same year, look in appendix C for the sign or signs that Saturn is in for that year or the closest prior year. If it is in any of the signs that challenge your luck, make note of those dates. If it is not in any of the signs that might challenge you, Saturn will not be a factor.

Putting It Together

Make note of your sun sign, Venus sign, Jupiter sign, and Saturn sign. Examine each planet as follows.

Example: Mr. D was born on March 22, 1960. His planets are as follows.

Sun is in Aries.
Venus is in Pisces.
Jupiter is in Capricorn.
Saturn is in Capricorn.

Luck is with him when:

Venus is in Pisces, Cancer, and Scorpio.
Jupiter is in Aries or Capricorn.

Saturn is not in Libra.
Luck is challenged when Saturn is in Aries, Cancer, or Capricorn.

In 2008, when are his lucky periods?

Venus is in Pisces, 3/12–4/5.
Venus is in Cancer, 6/18–7/11.
Venus is in Scorpio, 9/23–10/17.
Jupiter is in Capricorn for the entire year.
Saturn is in Virgo and does not affect luck this year.

Analysis: Because Jupiter is in Capricorn during 2008, the entire year should be lucky for Mr. D, but specific periods of good fortune are probably during the Venus periods.

Influence of the Moon

The moon changes sign every two and a half days. That means there are days every month when the moon is in the sign of your sun, Venus, Jupiter, and Saturn. The moon influences mood, emotion, and intuition. There are certain moon phases that can be significant in your relationship to luck.

Full moons and new moons can be considered wild cards. You can either test your luck or avoid risk when the full moon or new moon comes up in your sign. Here is a guide to the moon signs—look in your newspaper to see when the moon is full or new during that period and decide if you want to press your luck. For instance, if you are in a lucky period and there is a full moon in your sign, be cautious with your risks. The possibilities of great payoffs as well as reversals seem greater than on other days.

WHEN THE SUN IS IN	SIGN OF FULL MOON	SIGN OF NEW MOON
Aries 3/21–4/18	*Libra*	*Aries*
Taurus 4/19–5/19	*Scorpio*	*Taurus*
Gemini 5/19–6/19	*Sagittarius*	*Gemini*
Cancer 6/20–7/21	*Capricorn*	*Cancer*
Leo 7/22–8/21	*Aquarius*	*Leo*
Virgo 8/22–9/21	*Pisces*	*Virgo*
Libra 9/22–10/21	*Aries*	*Libra*
Scorpio 10/22–11/20	*Taurus*	*Scorpio*
Sagittarius 11/21–12/20	*Gemini*	*Sagittarius*
Capricorn 12/21–1/19	*Cancer*	*Capricorn*
Aquarius 1/20–2/18	*Leo*	*Aquarius*
Pisces 2/19–3/19	*Virgo*	*Pisces*

Applying Numerology: Your Personal Numbers

Here are the basic tools with which you can identify your personal numbers. Look over various meanings and see what resonates for you—what *feels* right usually *is* right.

Numbers of Your Life

The first place you can look for numbers is in the date of your birth. Add the digits that make up your birthday. For Mr. D, it's 3/22/1960. You can add the numbers in any combination and you'll always end up with the same *reduced* one-digit number.

Your one-digit number is what is called your "life number." You will always "be" that number, just as you will always be your astrological sign.

REDUCING A BIRTHDAY— EXAMPLE: MARCH 22, 1960

Method 1.

3 + 22 + 1960 = 1985
1 + 9 + 8 + 5 = 23
2 + 3 = 5

Method 2.

3 + 2 + 2 + 1 + 9 + 6 + 0 = 23
2 + 3 = 5

The birthday of March 22, 1960, reveals a life number of 5.

EXCEPTIONS TO REDUCING YOUR LIFE NUMBER

If in reducing your personal number you find that you have an 11 or a 22, you don't have to reduce it any further. These are considered special life numbers and are defined separately.

WHAT YOUR LIFE NUMBER MEANS

Generally, life numbers may prove powerful and lucky throughout your lifetime. You should be sensitive to your life number and take advantage of opportunities to use it. Life numbers have the following general characteristics:

1—You operate as an independent spirit and must make decisions and choices on your own.

2—You have natural abilities to connect with people and to mediate, and your life will always involve others.

3—You possess a creative nature, and you need to be able to communicate to the world.

4—You are practical and responsible, and others will need your steady influence.

5—You need free rein. You are creative, impetuous, and mobile.

6—You are a natural healer and bring ease and comfort to the world.

7—You can synthesize incredible amounts of information and gain wisdom and spiritual growth.

8—You have the capacity for hard work that leads to material rewards.

9—You possess ever broadening acceptance and compassion and can share it with the world.

11—You have a great deal of spiritual and intuitive insight and can channel these resources to help the world.

22—You are a big thinker and one who can tackle large-scale problems with success.

USING YOUR LIFE NUMBER TO DETERMINE YOUR PERSONAL YEAR NUMBER

Now that you are familiar with your personal life number, you can use it to figure out lucky phases. Every year heralds a new personal year number. All you need to do is add the current year to your life number and see where that takes you.

Life Number + Year Number = Personal Year Number

HOW TO DETERMINE THE PERSONAL YEAR NUMBER

Take the year you want to examine—for instance, the year 2008. The year number is determined by adding the digits of the year.

$2 + 0 + 0 + 8 = 10$ and $1 + 0 = 1$

The year 2008 is a "1" year, a year of new beginnings. Since it is an election year in the United States, the year will introduce new leaders.

APPLYING THE YEAR NUMBER TO YOUR LIFE NUMBER

Mr. D, who is a 5, can determine his personal year number as follows:

Life Number 5 + Year Number 1 = Personal Year Number 6

During 2008, Mr. D will have a 6 year, which according to the story of numbers in chapter 5, is one of harmony and good luck. Mr. D could also just take the number 6 at face value and use it as a special number during the year.

MONTH-BY-MONTH AND DAY-BY-DAY NUMBERS

Some numerologists take life numbers down to a monthly and even a daily level. You can do this by adding any date to your life number. If you have something important going on or you have an event on a certain date, you can check your personal date number to see if your luck will be challenged or enhanced. Here are a few examples of how to do this:

Life Number +	Date =	Personal Date Number
6	5/20/2009 5 + 2 + 2 + 9 = 18 1 + 8 = 9	6 + 9 = 15 1 + 5 = 6

According to the story of numbers in chapter 5, the number 6 is interpreted as follows: On this day, you will find harmony and good luck.

WHAT'S LUCKY?

These interpretations are broad and give only a general theme to the time of the calculation. It's important for you to look at the numbers through the lens of your experience. If you have a connection to the number 5 and you find that you have a 5 day or a 5 month, it can be lucky for you. Using numerology demands that you filter through the techniques for calculation and find the way it works best for you based on your own experience.

NUMBERS THROUGH LETTERS

As if there weren't enough to do in numerology already, add to the mix interpreting words and letters. Every word on this page has a numerical value. People have been associating number values to alphabets for thousands of years.

In Kabala, ancient Jewish mysticism, numbers are extremely important. Each Hebrew letter has a numerical value, and every word in the language—and your name—can be reduced. Numerical associations in Kabala don't always match up to Western numerology. For instance, in Hebrew the word for "life" is *chai.* In Hebrew numerology, or Gematria, the letters that spell that word add up to 18, and therefore 18 is a lucky number. In what we covered previously in modern Western numerology, 18 is a number that needs to be reduced to 1 + 8 = 9, which is usually about the end of the cycle of numbers.

For purposes of your luck, it's worth looking into what numbers mean across all cultures. Since you're reading this in

English, you're probably best off interpreting your name in this Western system.

LETTERS BY NUMBERS

Every letter of the alphabet can be associated with a number. You can interpret your name, your street, your town—any single thing that is written in letters can be "translated" into numbers.

Once you have the numerical translation of each letter, you reduce the entire equation to a single number. That's the number you can interpret.

Following is the key to letters by number and an example of reducing a word into a single number.

A	*B*	*C*	*D*	*E*	*F*	*G*	*H*	*I*	*J*	*K*
1	*2*	*3*	*4*	*5*	*6*	*7*	*8*	*9*	*10*	*11*
L	*M*	*N*	*O*	*P*	*Q*	*R*	*S*	*T*		
12	*13*	*14*	*15*	*16*	*17*	*18*	*19*	*20*		
U	*V*	*W*	*X*	*Y*	*Z*					
21	*22*	*23*	*24*	*25*	*26*					

GOOGLE

G = *7*
O = *15*
O = *15*

G = *7*
L = *12*
E = *5*

7 + 15 + 15 + 7 + 12 + 5 = 61
6 + 1 = 7

Google is a 7. According to the story of numbers in chapter 5, the number 7 is associated with gambling and risk. As a life number, it is an entity that can synthesize great amounts of wisdom and be open to spiritual growth. It has also historically been a lucky number.

Is it a coincidence that Google is so successful? Or is it riding the luck of numbers?

It's almost too easy to interpret every single thing in your life by numbers. Your name, your street address, your boss, your friends—it can get overwhelming. The best way to use this sort of information is sparingly.

Look at your initials, your nickname, and your legal name. You can also look at your address. Perhaps look at your life and see if there is a name that has appeared frequently—you can always decipher its numerical meaning.

HOW TO DECIDE WHAT NUMBERS ARE YOUR NUMBERS

Here's where the little voice in your head or that feeling in your gut is important. What feels right to you? There are so many associations for different numbers, it is not possible to say which is right. On the following pages, we provide different interpretations of numbers and their meaning. See how your numbers work for you.

MEANINGS OF NUMBERS IN CHINESE BELIEFS

1—Unity.
2—Balance/symmetry.
3—Lucky because it sounds like "ever growing."
4—Unlucky because it sounds like the word for death.
5—The self, me, myself, stands for completeness.
6—Going smoothly, sounds like "good luck" in Cantonese.
7—Together.
8—Sudden fortune, prosperity.
9—Long in time.

Some lucky number combinations include the following:

168—Road of prosperity.
518—I will prosper; other variations include 5189 (I will prosper for a long time), 516289 (I will get on a long, smooth, prosperous road), and 5918 (I will soon prosper).
888—Prosperity × 3.

NUMBERS 1 TO 10 IN KABALA: THE TREE OF LIFE	
1. *Keter*/Crown, Unknowable Spirit:	The Tree's Roots
2. *Chochmah*/Wisdom	The Tree's Trunk and Branches
3. *Binah*/Understanding	
4. *Chesed*/Expanse	
5. *Guvurah*/Limits	
6. *Tiferet*/Beauty	
7. *Netzach*/Initiative	
8. *Hod*/Surrender	
9. *Yesod*/Foundation	
10. *Malkhut*/Earth:	The Tree's Fruits

(The Tree's Trunk and Branches applies to items 2–9.)

NUMERICAL ASSOCIATIONS IN ASTROLOGY

NUMBER	PLANET	SIGN
1	*Sun*	*Leo*
2	*Moon*	*Cancer*
3	*Jupiter*	*Sagittarius*
4	*Uranus*	*Aquarius*
5	*Mercury*	*Gemini, Virgo*
6	*Venus*	*Taurus, Libra*
7	*Neptune*	*Pisces*
8	*Saturn*	*Capricorn*
9	*Mars*	*Aries, Scorpio*

Applying Tarot

As you know, tarot cards became very popular in pre-Renaissance Italy. The meanings assigned to the cards are relatively unchanged, but since language and symbols evolve over time, it can be difficult to find the core meaning of the card at first glance. Here is a way to use tarot cards to give you insight into your luck. If you have a tarot deck, simply pull a card from the deck randomly and look at the symbol. You can pull a card for any topic at any time. Ask about a pet project or how you'll do at the casino. If you happen to pull a card that says "strength," it would imply that moving forward with integrity is important.

This is a look at how traditional tarot cards can be used to give you insight into whether or not luck will be on your side. Especially lucky tarot cards are the Empress, Emperor, Chariot, Lovers, Strength, Star, Sun, and The World.

NUMBER	TRADITIONAL NAME	REINTERPRETED
0	*Fool*	*Raw Potential*
1	*Magician*	*Inventiveness*
2	*Virgin*	*Something Coming Soon*
3	*Empress*	*Feminine Power*
4	*Emperor*	*Masculine Power*
5	*Hierophant*	*Traditional Paths*
6	*Lovers*	*Lovers/Important Pair*
7	*Chariot*	*Ambition/Triumph*
8	*Strength*	*Strength/Integrity*
9	*Hermit*	*Willpower*
10	*Wheel of Fortune*	*Fate/Destiny*
11	*Justice*	*Justice*
12	*Hanged Man*	*Insecurity*
13	*Death*	*Transformation*
14	*Temperance*	*Moderation*
15	*Devil*	*Temptation*
16	*Tower*	*Disruption*
17	*Star*	*Hope*
18	*Moon*	*Mystery*
19	*Sun*	*Vitality*
20	*Judgment*	*Forgiveness*
21	*The World*	*Success*

If you pull a card that is from the Minor Arcana, read the following interpretations for insight.

MINOR ARCANA	
CUPS — WATER	**REINTERPRETED**
1	*Hopefulness*
2	*Attraction*
3	*Good connection*
4	*Same old security*
5	*Upset*
6	*Relief*
7	*Flirtatious*
8	*Ease up*
9	*All is well*
10	*Let it end*
Knave	*Seer*
Prince	*Sensor*
Queen	*Nurturer*
King	*Listener*
COINS OR PENTACLES — EARTH	**REINTERPRETED**
1	*A new beginning*
2	*Growth potential*
3	*Growth*
4	*Stability*
5	*Challenge*
6	*Harmony*
7	*Risk*

(CONTINUED)

COINS OR PENTACLES—EARTH	REINTERPRETED
8	*Perseverance*
9	*Abundance*
10	*Rationing*
Knave	*Scout*
Prince	*Sport*
Queen	*Guide*
King	*Master*

WANDS—FIRE	REINTERPRETED
1	*Take initiative*
2	*Feel the passion*
3	*Work hard*
4	*Complete the task*
5	*Compete*
6	*Be recognized*
7	*Rebel*
8	*Get enthused*
9	*Be a star*
10	*Download*
Knave	*Adventurer*
Prince	*Explorer*
Queen	*Creator*
King	*Commander*

SWORDS — AIR	REINTERPRETED
1	*Be open to new ideas*
2	*There's a possibility*
3	*Is this real?*
4	*Use logic*
5	*Argue and defend*
6	*Reach new understanding*
7	*Explore new approaches*
8	*Review the past*
9	*I get it!*
10	*Think it over*
Knave	*Reporter*
Prince	*Analyst*
Queen	*Knower*
King	*Leader*

Applying Time

Luck is all in the timing. You can play with time yourself by using the following information. Remember, luck doesn't like to be pinned down, so these are only guidelines—luck likes the unexpected. Will these days or hours work for you? You won't know until you try.

According to antiquities expert Wallis Budge, in the Middle Ages it was believed that lucky days were Sunday, Monday, Wednesday, and Thursday. Certain hours of the day were also assigned luck.

LUCKY HOURS OF THE DAY

SUNDAY	*3:00 P.M.–4:30 P.M.*
MONDAY	*1:00 P.M.–3:00 P.M.*
TUESDAY	*Noon–3:30 P.M.*
WEDNESDAY	*10:00 A.M.–noon*

THURSDAY	*9:00 A.M.–10:30 A.M.*
FRIDAY	*7:00 A.M.–9:00 A.M.*
SATURDAY	*6:00 A.M.–7:30 A.M.*

LUCKY HOURS OF THE NIGHT

According to Scott Cunningham's *Magical Herbalism*, night starts at sunset and ends at sunrise. Take the time between sunset and sunrise, divide into twelve equal parts, and you'll have the exact hours. Lucky hours of the night are as follows:

Sunday: first hour, eighth hour
Monday: fifth hour, twelfth hour
Tuesday: second hour, ninth hour
Wednesday: sixth hour
Thursday: third hour, tenth hour
Friday: seventh hour
Saturday: fourth hour, eleventh hour

Applying Herbs

As we've seen, nature plays an enormous role in what is considered lucky. Taken from Scott Cunningham's *Cunningham's Encyclopedia of Magical Herbs*, here is a summary of herbs and their lucky powers. You might want to try some out in your garden or in a sachet that you can carry.

Allspice—The incense is burned for luck.

Aloe—In Mexico, it is made into wreaths for luck and protection.

Cabbage—Plant this after marriage for a lucky union.

Chinese bamboo—Put this over a doorway.

Corn—From North American and Eastern cultures, hang stalks over a mirror for good luck.

Daffodil—Pluck it and wear it next to your heart for good luck.

Fern—The person who breaks the first fern frond of spring will have good luck.

Hazelnuts—Hang in the house for good luck.

Holly—Good luck at yule; men carry it for good luck.

Irish moss—Place it underneath rugs for a steady flow of money.

Job's tears—Carry three seeds for good luck.

Linden trees—Carve a good-luck charm from this wood.

Moss—The moss from a gravestone is good luck.

Nutmeg—A whole nutmeg carried brings good luck.

Orange—Symbol of good luck.

Persimmon—Buy a green persimmon for good luck.

Pineapple—Add dried pineapple to a bath for good luck.

Pomegranate—Make a wish before you eat it. The plentiful seeds bring many opportunities for luck.

Poppy seeds—Eat or carry them with you for fertile good luck.

Purslane—Carried, it brings good luck.

Star anise—Carry for luck.

Strawberry leaves—Also carry for good luck.

Violet—Carry this to change your luck.

Applying Colors

Some people have to wear their lucky orange shirt or fuzzy brown socks. Colors can play a big part in luck either by accident or on purpose. Here are the general meanings of colors. Would you change anything about what colors you wear knowing this? You have a rainbow of colors to choose from. Of course, you can mix and blend them for different effects.

Red is the color of blood, war, roses, love, passion, a vital force (as in the Red Cross). It is associated with the root chakra located at the base of your spine and below the pubic bones, also with the planet (and god of war) Mars.

Orange is a color that brings out emotional responses. Orange can portend success (like gold). It's a color associated with harmony, pride, ambition, and strength. It is associated with the lower or navel chakra, just beneath your belly button. Orange and yellow are Leo and sun colors.

Yellow is the sun and vitality, brightness and purification. But yellow has another side—it can mean cowardice as well.

Pink is a color associated with little girls and romantic idealism. If you have a big pink influence in your dreams, consider what part of your life is still influenced by your hopeful, idealistic youth.

Green is a color of life and abundance (which is why our money is green). That's the positive side. Green also means mold and slime—so make sure you have a sense of how that green in your dream made you feel.

Blue is a spiritual color. It's pure, clear, and calm. Blue in dreams can be a sign of an important spiritual message. Conversely, blue can mean depression, as in "having the blues."

Purple is a royal color. Generally, it's a good dream color because it indicates dominance or success for you. However, too much of a good thing can lead to pomposity or excess.

Brown is earthiness and stability. Brown is also the color of excrement, which can mean abundance (the good) and filth (the bad).

Gray is a middle tone. Since it rests between black and white, what you've got here is a transition, neither good nor bad.

White is a spiritual and ritualistic color that we associate with purity. Strong white color in your dreams would most likely give you a feeling of open space and possibility, the infinity of spirit. It can also mean emptiness, which is the same thing, only somewhat negative.

Black is the color of mystery. It's the unknown, the unconscious. Black is a sacred color and can indicate the gestation of a new part of you. Black also represents your fears, mourning, or destruction.

IF YOU WERE BORN ON A	WEAR THIS FOR GOOD LUCK
SUNDAY	*Gold*
MONDAY	*Silver and crescents*
TUESDAY	*Red*
WEDNESDAY	*Blue*
THURSDAY	*Ankh or a cross*
FRIDAY	*Diamonds*
SATURDAY	*Gold watch*

Applying Stones

Lucky stones are typically green in color. Green is associated with life and prosperity. Some of the following stones are not green but are considered to have properties that attract abundance.

Aventurine (green)
Cat's-eye (varying shades of gold and brown)
Mint green (chrysoprase)
Emerald (green)
Garnet (deep red)
Jade (Chinese)
Lapis lazuli (ancient Sumer) (blue with specks of gold)
Malachite (for business) (green)
Moonstone (in India) (milky white)
Turquoise (Native American and Islam)

LUCKY STONES BY MONTH

January—Garnet
February—Amethyst
March—Bloodstone
April—Diamond
May—Emerald
June—Agate
July—Turquoise
August—Carnelian
September—Chrysolite
October—Beryl
November—Topaz
December—Ruby

Applying Charms

Many people carry lucky charms with them on a daily basis. Whether it is a St. Christopher medal to protect luck in journeys or the letters that spell *chai*, the Hebrew word for "life," it's hard to resist the idea that these little helpers might make the difference in the way our days play out. Do you carry a good-luck charm? If you don't, just be on the lookout to see if one might come to you. Many of the items we covered in chapter 3 can be good-luck charms. Here are a few more good-luck charms from around the world:

Animal teeth—Some consider them lucky for gambling; shark's teeth are worn on necklaces for good luck.

Double happiness—This is a Chinese symbol of good luck, often given to couples on their wedding day.

Hamsa hand—In the Middle East, this is a charm for good luck and good health.

Kokopelli—Found in Native American culture, this is an image of a fun-loving character who can bring wealth.

Milagro—In Mexico, milagros are small charms that are worn or carried for good luck.

Penny—Find a penny, pick it up, and all the day you'll have good luck. (We always pick up pennies that are face up. If they are tails up, we turn them over and let someone else take the luck. The act of sharing luck is lucky, too.)

Pyramid—Placing one in your home can bring better energy and better luck.

Scarab—From Egypt, the scarab represents eternal life and good luck.

Two-dollar bill—They are considered rare and lucky in the United States.

Let a good-luck charm come to you. It might be a stone on a beach or a coin you find in your dresser. Whatever it is, let your charm approach you, and be smart enough—and lucky enough—to see it.

Personal Luck Profile Worksheet

Sun Sign: ______________________

Venus Sign: ______________________

Jupiter Sign: ______________________

Saturn Sign: ______________________

Life Number: ______________________

Year of Calculation: ______________________

Dates of Venus Luck: ______________________

Jupiter Luck: Yes/No

If so, date: ______________________

Saturn Challenge: Yes/No ______________________

If so, date: ______________________

Personal Year Number (Life Number + Year Number): ________

Lucky Herbs: ________

Lucky Colors: ________

Lucky Stones: ________

Lucky Charms: ________

Appendix A

VENUS IN THE SIGNS 1925–2017					
1925		1926		1927	
Jan 1	Sagittarius	Jan 1	Aquarius	Jan 1	Capricorn
Jan 14	Capricorn	Apr 5	Pisces	Jan 9	Aquarius
Feb 7	Aquarius	May 6	Aries	Feb 2	Pisces
Mar 3	Pisces	Jun 2	Taurus	Feb 26	Aries
Apr 21	Taurus	Jun 28	Gemini	Mar 22	Taurus
May 15	Gemini	Jul 24	Cancer	Apr 16	Gemini
Jun 8	Cancer	Aug 17	Leo	May 12	Cancer
Jul 28	Virgo	Sep 11	Virgo	Jun 7	Leo
Aug 21	Libra	Oct 5	Libra	Jul 7	Virgo
Sep 15	Scorpio	Oct 29	Scorpio	Nov 9	Libra
Oct 11	Sagittarius	Nov 22	Sagittarius	Dec 8	Scorpio
Nov 6	Capricorn	Dec 16	Capricorn		
Dec 5	Aquarius				

(CONTINUED)

1928		1929		1930	
Jan 1	Scorpio	Jan 1	Aquarius	Jan 1	Sagittarius
Jan 3	Sagittarius	Jan 6	Pisces	Jan 23	Aquarius
Jan 28	Capricorn	Feb 2	Aries	Feb 16	Pisces
Feb 22	Aquarius	Mar 8	Taurus	Mar 12	Aries
Mar 17	Pisces	Apr 19	Aries	Apr 5	Taurus
Apr 11	Aries	Jun 3	Taurus	Apr 30	Gemini
May 5	Taurus	Jul 7	Gemini	May 24	Cancer
May 30	Gemini	Aug 5	Cancer	Jun 18	Leo
Jun 23	Cancer	Aug 31	Leo	Jul 14	Virgo
Jul 18	Leo	Sep 25	Virgo	Aug 9	Libra
Aug 11	Virgo	Oct 20	Sagittarius	Sep 6	Scorpio
Sep 4	Libra	Nov 13	Libra	Oct 11	Sagittarius
Sep 29	Scorpio	Dec 7	Scorpio	Nov 22	Scorpio
Oct 23	Sagittarius	Dec 30	Sagittarius		
Nov 17	Capricorn				
Dec 11	Aquarius				

1931		1932		1933	
Jan 1	Scorpio	Jan 1	Aquarius	Jan 1	Sagittarius
Jan 3	Sagittarius	Jan 18	Pisces	Jan 14	Capricorn
Feb 6	Capricorn	Feb 12	Aries	Feb 7	Aquarius
Mar 5	Aquarius	Mar 8	Taurus	Mar 3	Pisces
Mar 31	Pisces	Apr 4	Gemini	Mar 27	Aries
Apr 25	Aries	May 6	Cancer	Apr 20	Taurus
May 20	Taurus	Jul 13	Gemini	May 14	Gemini
Jun 14	Gemini	Jul 28	Cancer	Jun 8	Cancer
Jul 9	Cancer	Sep 8	Leo	Jul 2	Leo

1931		1932		1933	
Aug 2	Leo	Oct 7	Virgo	Jul 27	Virgo
Aug 27	Virgo	Nov 1	Libra	Aug 21	Libra
Sep 20	Libra	Nov 26	Scorpio	Sep 15	Scorpio
Oct 14	Scorpio	Dec 21	Sagittarius	Oct 10	Sagittarius
Nov 7	Sagittarius			Nov 6	Capricorn
Dec 1	Capricorn			Dec 5	Aquarius
Dec 25	Aquarius				

1934		1935		1936	
Jan 1	Aquarius	Jan 1	Capricorn	Jan 1	Scorpio
Apr 6	Pisces	Jan 8	Aquarius	Jan 3	Sagittarius
May 6	Aries	Feb 1	Pisces	Jan 28	Capricorn
Jun 2	Taurus	Feb 25	Aries	Feb 21	Aquarius
Jun 28	Gemini	Mar 22	Taurus	Mar 17	Pisces
Jul 23	Cancer	Apr 16	Gemini	Apr 10	Aries
Aug 17	Leo	May 11	Cancer	May 5	Taurus
Sep 10	Virgo	Jun 7	Leo	May 29	Gemini
Oct 5	Libra	Jul 7	Virgo	Jun 23	Cancer
Oct 29	Scorpio	Nov 9	Libra	Jul 17	Leo
Nov 21	Sagittarius	Dec 8	Scorpio	Aug 10	Virgo
Dec 15	Capricorn			Sep 4	Libra
				Sep 28	Scorpio
				Oct 23	Sagittarius
				Nov 16	Capricorn
				Dec 11	Aquarius

(CONTINUED)

1937		1938		1939	
Jan 1	Aquarius	Jan 1	Capricorn	Jan 1	Scorpio
Jan 5	Pisces	Jan 23	Aquarius	Jan 4	Sagittarius
Feb 2	Aries	Feb 16	Pisces	Feb 6	Capricorn
Mar 9	Taurus	Mar 12	Aries	Mar 5	Aquarius
Apr 13	Aries	Apr 5	Taurus	Mar 31	Pisces
Jun 4	Taurus	Apr 29	Gemini	Apr 25	Aries
Jul 7	Gemini	May 24	Cancer	May 20	Taurus
Aug 4	Cancer	Jun 18	Leo	Jun 14	Gemini
Aug 30	Leo	Jul 14	Virgo	Jul 8	Cancer
Sep 24	Virgo	Aug 9	Libra	Aug 2	Leo
Oct 19	Libra	Sep 6	Scorpio	Aug 26	Virgo
Nov 12	Scorpio	Oct 13	Sagittarius	Sep 19	Libra
Dec 6	Sagittarius	Nov 15	Scorpio	Oct 13	Scorpio
Dec 30	Capricorn			Nov 6	Sagittarius
				Nov 30	Capricorn
				Dec 25	Aquarius

1940		1941		1942	
Jan 1	Aquarius	Jan 1	Sagittarius	Jan 1	Aquarius
Jan 18	Pisces	Jan 13	Capricorn	Apr 6	Pisces
Feb 12	Aries	Feb 6	Aquarius	May 5	Aries
Mar 8	Taurus	Mar 2	Pisces	Jun 1	Taurus
Apr 4	Gemini	Mar 26	Aries	Jun 27	Gemini
May 6	Cancer	Apr 20	Taurus	Jul 23	Cancer
Jul 5	Gemini	May 14	Gemini	Aug 16	Leo
Jul 31	Cancer	Jun 7	Cancer	Sep 10	Virgo
Sep 8	Leo	Jul 2	Leo	Oct 4	Libra

1940		1941		1942	
Oct 6	Virgo	Jul 26	Virgo	Oct 28	Scorpio
Nov 1	Libra	Aug 20	Libra	Nov 21	Sagittarius
Nov 26	Scorpio	Sep 14	Scorpio	Dec 15	Capricorn
Dec 20	Sagittarius	Oct 10	Sagittarius		
		Nov 6	Capricorn		
		Dec 5	Aquarius		

1943		1944		1945	
Jan 1	Capricorn	Jan 1	Scorpio	Jan 1	Aquarius
Jan 8	Aquarius	Jan 2	Sagittarius	Jan 5	Pisces
Feb 1	Pisces	Jan 27	Capricorn	Feb 2	Aries
Feb 25	Aries	Feb 21	Aquarius	Mar 11	Taurus
Mar 21	Taurus	Mar 16	Pisces	Apr 7	Aries
Apr 15	Gemini	Apr 10	Aries	Jun 4	Taurus
May 11	Cancer	May 4	Taurus	Jul 7	Gemini
Jun 7	Leo	May 29	Gemini	Aug 4	Cancer
Jul 7	Virgo	Jun 22	Cancer	Aug 30	Leo
Nov 9	Libra	Jul 16	Leo	Sep 24	Virgo
Dec 8	Scorpio	Aug 10	Virgo	Oct 18	Libra
		Sep 3	Libra	Nov 12	Scorpio
		Sep 28	Scorpio	Dec 6	Sagittarius
		Oct 22	Sagittarius	Dec 29	Capricorn
		Nov 16	Capricorn		
		Dec 10	Aquarius		

(CONTINUED)

1946		1947		1948	
Jan 1	Capricorn	Jan 1	Scorpio	Jan 1	Aquarius
Jan 22	Aquarius	Jan 5	Sagittarius	Jan 17	Pisces
Feb 15	Pisces	Feb 6	Capricorn	Feb 11	Aries
Mar 11	Aries	Mar 5	Aquarius	Mar 8	Taurus
Apr 4	Taurus	Mar 30	Pisces	Apr 4	Gemini
Apr 29	Gemini	Apr 24	Aries	May 7	Cancer
May 23	Cancer	May 19	Taurus	Jun 29	Gemini
Jun 18	Leo	Jun 13	Gemini	Aug 2	Cancer
Jul 13	Virgo	Jul 8	Cancer	Sep 8	Leo
Aug 9	Libra	Aug 1	Leo	Oct 6	Virgo
Sep 6	Scorpio	Aug 26	Virgo	Nov 1	Libra
Oct 16	Sagittarius	Sep 19	Libra	Nov 25	Scorpio
Nov 8	Scorpio	Oct 13	Scorpio	Dec 20	Sagittarius
		Nov 6	Sagittarius		
		Nov 30	Capricorn		
		Dec 24	Aquarius		

1949		1950		1951	
Jan 1	Sagittarius	Jan 1	Aquarius	Jan 1	Capricorn
Jan 13	Capricorn	Apr 6	Pisces	Jan 7	Aquarius
Feb 6	Aquarius	May 5	Aries	Jan 31	Pisces
Mar 2	Pisces	Jun 1	Taurus	Feb 24	Aries
Mar 26	Aries	Jun 27	Gemini	Mar 21	Taurus
Apr 19	Taurus	Jul 22	Cancer	Apr 15	Gemini
May 13	Gemini	Aug 16	Leo	May 10	Cancer
Jun 7	Cancer	Sep 9	Virgo	Jun 7	Leo
Jul 1	Leo	Oct 4	Libra	Jul 7	Virgo

1949		1950		1951	
Aug 20	Virgo	Oct 28	Scorpio	Nov 9	Libra
Sep 14	Libra	Nov 20	Sagittarius	Dec 7	Scorpio
Oct 10	Sagittarius	Dec 14	Capricorn		
Nov 5	Capricorn				
Dec 6	Aquarius				

1952		1953		1954	
Jan 1	Scorpio	Jan 1	Aquarius	Jan 1	Capricorn
Jan 2	Sagittarius	Jan 5	Pisces	Jan 22	Aquarius
Jan 27	Capricorn	Feb 2	Aries	Feb 15	Pisces
Feb 20	Aquarius	Mar 14	Taurus	Mar 11	Aries
Mar 16	Pisces	Mar 31	Aries	Apr 4	Taurus
Apr 9	Aries	Jun 5	Taurus	Apr 28	Gemini
May 4	Taurus	Jul 7	Gemini	May 23	Cancer
May 28	Gemini	Aug 3	Cancer	Jun 17	Leo
Jun 22	Cancer	Aug 29	Leo	Jul 13	Virgo
Jul 16	Leo	Sep 23	Virgo	Aug 8	Libra
Aug 9	Virgo	Oct 18	Libra	Sep 6	Scorpio
Sep 3	Libra	Nov 11	Scorpio	Oct 23	Sagittarius
Sep 27	Scorpio	Dec 5	Sagittarius	Oct 27	Scorpio
Oct 22	Sagittarius	Dec 29	Capricorn		
Nov 15	Capricorn				
Dec 10	Aquarius				

(CONTINUED)

1955		1956		1957	
Jan 1	Scorpio	Jan 1	Aquarius	Jan 1	Sagittarius
Jan 6	Sagittarius	Jan 17	Pisces	Jan 12	Capricorn
Feb 5	Capricorn	Feb 11	Aries	Feb 5	Aquarius
Mar 4	Aquarius	Mar 7	Taurus	Mar 1	Pisces
Mar 30	Pisces	Apr 4	Gemini	Mar 25	Aries
Apr 24	Aries	May 7	Cancer	Apr 18	Taurus
May 19	Taurus	Jun 23	Gemini	May 13	Gemini
Jun 13	Gemini	Aug 4	Cancer	Jun 6	Cancer
Jul 7	Cancer	Sep 8	Leo	Jul 1	Leo
Aug 1	Leo	Oct 5	Virgo	Jul 25	Virgo
Aug 25	Virgo	Oct 31	Libra	Aug 19	Libra
Sep 18	Libra	Nov 25	Scorpio	Sep 14	Scorpio
Oct 12	Scorpio	Dec 19	Sagittarius	Oct 9	Sagittarius
Nov 5	Sagittarius			Nov 5	Capricorn
Nov 29	Capricorn			Dec 6	Aquarius
Dec 24	Aquarius				

1958		1959		1960	
Jan 1	Aquarius	Jan 1	Capricorn	Jan 1	Scorpio
Apr 6	Pisces	Jan 7	Aquarius	Jan 2	Sagittarius
May 5	Aries	Jan 31	Pisces	Jan 26	Capricorn
May 31	Taurus	Feb 24	Aries	Feb 20	Aquarius
Jun 26	Gemini	Mar 20	Taurus	Mar 15	Pisces
Jul 22	Cancer	Apr 14	Gemini	Apr 9	Aries
Aug 15	Leo	May 10	Cancer	May 3	Taurus
Sep 9	Virgo	Jun 6	Leo	May 28	Gemini
Oct 3	Libra	Jul 8	Virgo	Jun 21	Cancer

1958		1959		1960	
Oct 27	Scorpio	Sep 19	Leo	Jul 15	Leo
Nov 20	Sagittarius	Sep 25	Virgo	Aug 9	Virgo
Dec 14	Capricorn	Nov 9	Libra	Sep 2	Libra
		Dec 7	Scorpio	Sep 27	Scorpio
				Oct 21	Sagittarius
				Nov 15	Capricorn
				Dec 10	Aquarius

1961		1962		1963	
Jan 1	Aquarius	Jan 1	Capricorn	Jan 1	Scorpio
Jan 4	Capricorn	Jan 21	Aquarius	Jan 6	Sagittarius
Feb 1	Aries	Feb 14	Pisces	Feb 5	Capricorn
Jun 5	Taurus	Mar 10	Aries	Mar 4	Aquarius
Jul 6	Gemini	Apr 3	Taurus	Mar 29	Pisces
Aug 3	Cancer	Apr 28	Gemini	Apr 23	Aries
Aug 29	Leo	May 22	Cancer	May 18	Taurus
Sep 23	Virgo	Jun 17	Leo	Jun 12	Gemini
Oct 17	Libra	Jul 12	Virgo	Jul 7	Cancer
Nov 11	Scorpio	Aug 8	Libra	Jul 31	Leo
Dec 4	Sagittarius	Sep 6	Scorpio	Aug 25	Virgo
Dec 28	Capricorn			Sep 18	Libra
				Oct 12	Scorpio
				Nov 5	Sagittarius
				Nov 29	Capricorn
				Dec 23	Aquarius

(CONTINUED)

1964		1965		1966	
Jan 1	Aquarius	Jan 1	Sagittarius	Jan 1	Aquarius
Jan 16	Pisces	Jan 12	Capricorn	Feb 6	Capricorn
Feb 10	Aries	Feb 5	Aquarius	Feb 25	Aquarius
Mar 7	Taurus	Mar 1	Pisces	Apr 6	Pisces
Apr 3	Gemini	Mar 25	Aries	May 4	Aries
May 8	Cancer	Apr 18	Taurus	May 31	Taurus
Jun 17	Gemini	May 12	Gemini	Jun 26	Gemini
Aug 5	Cancer	Jun 6	Cancer	Jul 21	Cancer
Sep 7	Leo	Jun 30	Leo	Aug 15	Leo
Oct 5	Virgo	Jul 25	Virgo	Sep 8	Virgo
Oct 31	Libra	Aug 19	Libra	Oct 2	Libra
Nov 24	Scorpio	Sep 13	Scorpio	Oct 26	Scorpio
Dec 19	Sagittarius	Oct 9	Sagittarius	Nov 19	Sagittarius
		Nov 5	Capricorn	Dec 13	Capricorn
		Dec 6	Aquarius		

1967		1968		1969	
Jan 1	Capricorn	Jan 1	Sagittarius	Jan 1	Aquarius
Jan 6	Aquarius	Jan 26	Capricorn	Jan 4	Pisces
Jan 30	Pisces	Feb 19	Aquarius	Feb 1	Aries
Feb 23	Aries	Mar 15	Pisces	Jun 5	Taurus
Mar 20	Taurus	Apr 8	Aries	Jul 6	Gemini
Apr 14	Gemini	May 3	Taurus	Aug 3	Cancer
May 10	Cancer	May 27	Gemini	Aug 28	Leo
Jun 6	Leo	Jun 20	Cancer	Sep 22	Virgo
Jul 8	Virgo	Jul 15	Leo	Oct 17	Libra
Sep 9	Leo	Aug 8	Virgo	Nov 10	Scorpio

1967		1968		1969	
Oct 1	Virgo	Sep 2	Libra	Dec 4	Sagittarius
Nov 9	Libra	Sep 26	Scorpio	Dec 28	Capricorn
Dec 7	Scorpio	Oct 21	Sagittarius		
		Nov 14	Capricorn		
		Dec 9	Aquarius		

1970		1971		1972	
Jan 1	Capricorn	Jan 1	Scorpio	Jan 1	Aquarius
Jan 21	Aquarius	Jan 6	Sagittarius	Jan 16	Pisces
Feb 14	Pisces	Feb 5	Capricorn	Feb 10	Aries
Mar 10	Aries	Mar 3	Aquarius	Mar 6	Taurus
Apr 3	Taurus	Mar 29	Pisces	Apr 3	Gemini
Apr 27	Gemini	Apr 23	Aries	May 10	Cancer
May 22	Cancer	May 18	Taurus	Jun 11	Gemini
Jun 16	Leo	Jun 12	Gemini	Aug 5	Cancer
Jul 12	Virgo	Jul 6	Cancer	Sep 7	Leo
Aug 8	Libra	Jul 31	Leo	Oct 5	Virgo
Sep 6	Scorpio	Aug 24	Virgo	Oct 30	Libra
		Sep 17	Libra	Nov 24	Scorpio
		Oct 11	Scorpio	Dec 18	Sagittarius
		Nov 4	Sagittarius		
		Nov 28	Capricorn		
		Dec 23	Aquarius		

(CONTINUED)

1973		1974		1975	
Jan 1	Sagittarius	Jan 1	Aquarius	Jan 1	Capricorn
Jan 11	Capricorn	Jan 29	Capricorn	Jan 6	Aquarius
Feb 4	Aquarius	Feb 28	Aquarius	Jan 30	Pisces
Feb 28	Pisces	Apr 6	Pisces	Feb 23	Aries
Mar 24	Aries	May 4	Aries	Mar 19	Taurus
Apr 17	Taurus	May 31	Taurus	Apr 13	Gemini
May 12	Gemini	Jun 25	Gemini	May 9	Cancer
Jun 5	Cancer	Jul 20	Cancer	Jun 6	Leo
Jun 30	Leo	Aug 14	Leo	Jul 9	Virgo
Jul 24	Virgo	Sep 8	Virgo	Sep 2	Leo
Aug 18	Libra	Oct 2	Libra	Oct 4	Virgo
Sep 13	Scorpio	Oct 26	Scorpio	Nov 9	Libra
Oct 9	Sagittarius	Nov 19	Sagittarius	Dec 6	Scorpio
Nov 5	Capricorn	Dec 13	Capricorn		
Dec 7	Aquarius				

1976		1977		1978	
Jan 1	Sagittarius	Jan 1	Aquarius	Jan 1	Capricorn
Jan 26	Capricorn	Jan 4	Pisces	Jan 20	Aquarius
Feb 19	Aquarius	Feb 2	Aries	Feb 13	Pisces
Mar 14	Pisces	Jun 6	Taurus	Mar 9	Aries
Apr 8	Aries	Jul 6	Gemini	Apr 2	Taurus
May 2	Taurus	Aug 2	Cancer	Apr 27	Gemini
May 26	Gemini	Aug 28	Leo	May 21	Cancer
Jun 20	Cancer	Sep 22	Virgo	Jun 16	Leo
Jul 14	Leo	Oct 16	Libra	Jul 11	Virgo
Aug 8	Virgo	Nov 9	Scorpio	Aug 7	Libra

1976		1977		1978	
Sep 1	Libra	Dec 3	Sagittarius	Sep 7	Scorpio
Sep 25	Scorpio	Dec 27	Capricorn		
Oct 20	Sagittarius				
Nov 14	Capricorn				
Dec 9	Sagittarius				

1979		1980		1981	
Jan 1	Scorpio	Jan 1	Aquarius	Jan 1	Sagittarius
Jan 7	Sagittarius	Jan 15	Pisces	Jan 11	Capricorn
Feb 5	Capricorn	Feb 9	Aries	Feb 4	Aquarius
Mar 3	Aquarius	Mar 6	Taurus	Feb 28	Pisces
Mar 28	Pisces	Apr 3	Gemini	Mar 24	Aries
Apr 22	Aries	May 12	Cancer	Apr 17	Taurus
May 17	Taurus	Jun 5	Gemini	May 11	Gemini
Jun 11	Gemini	Aug 6	Cancer	Jun 5	Cancer
Jul 6	Cancer	Sep 7	Leo	Jun 29	Leo
Jul 30	Leo	Oct 4	Virgo	Jul 24	Virgo
Aug 23	Virgo	Oct 30	Libra	Aug 18	Libra
Sep 17	Libra	Nov 23	Scorpio	Sep 12	Scorpio
Oct 11	Scorpio	Dec 18	Sagittarius	Oct 8	Sagittarius
Nov 4	Sagittarius			Nov 5	Capricorn
Nov 28	Capricorn			Dec 8	Aquarius
Dec 22	Aquarius				

(CONTINUED)

1982		1983		1984	
Jan 1	Aquarius	Jan 1	Capricorn	Jan 1	Sagittarius
Jan 22	Capricorn	Jan 5	Aquarius	Jan 25	Capricorn
Mar 2	Aquarius	Jan 29	Pisces	Feb 18	Aquarius
Apr 6	Pisces	Feb 22	Aries	Mar 14	Pisces
May 4	Aries	Mar 19	Taurus	Apr 7	Aries
Jun 25	Gemini	Apr 13	Gemini	May 1	Taurus
Jul 20	Cancer	May 9	Cancer	May 26	Gemini
Aug 14	Leo	Jun 6	Leo	Jun 19	Cancer
Sep 7	Virgo	Jul 10	Virgo	Jul 14	Leo
Oct 1	Libra	Aug 27	Leo	Aug 7	Virgo
Oct 25	Scorpio	Oct 5	Virgo	Sep 1	Libra
Nov 18	Sagittarius	Nov 9	Libra	Sep 25	Scorpio
Dec 12	Capricorn	Dec 6	Scorpio	Oct 20	Sagittarius
		Dec 31	Sagittarius	Nov 13	Capricorn
				Dec 8	Aquarius

1985		1986		1987	
Jan 1	Aquarius	Jan 1	Capricorn	Jan 1	Scorpio
Jan 4	Pisces	Jan 20	Aquarius	Jan 7	Sagittarius
Feb 2	Aries	Feb 12	Pisces	Feb 4	Capricorn
Jun 6	Taurus	Mar 8	Aries	Mar 3	Aquarius
Jul 6	Gemini	Apr 2	Taurus	Mar 28	Pisces
Aug 2	Cancer	Apr 26	Gemini	Apr 22	Aries
Aug 27	Leo	May 21	Cancer	May 17	Taurus
Sep 21	Virgo	Jun 15	Leo	Jun 11	Gemini
Oct 16	Libra	Jul 11	Virgo	Jul 5	Cancer
Nov 9	Scorpio	Aug 7	Libra	Jul 30	Leo

1985		1986		1987	
Dec 3	Sagittarius	Sep 7	Scorpio	Aug 23	Virgo
Dec 27	Capricorn			Sep 16	Libra
				Oct 10	Scorpio
				Nov 3	Sagittarius
				Nov 27	Capricorn
				Dec 22	Aquarius

1988		1989		1990	
Jan 1	Aquarius	Jan 1	Sagittarius	Jan 1	Aquarius
Jan 15	Pisces	Jan 10	Capricorn	Jan 16	Capricorn
Feb 9	Aries	Feb 3	Aquarius	Mar 3	Aquarius
Mar 6	Taurus	Feb 27	Pisces	Apr 6	Pisces
Apr 3	Gemini	Mar 23	Aries	May 3	Aries
May 17	Cancer	Apr 16	Taurus	May 30	Taurus
May 27	Gemini	May 11	Gemini	Jun 24	Gemini
Aug 6	Cancer	Jun 4	Cancer	Jul 19	Cancer
Sep 7	Leo	Jun 29	Leo	Aug 13	Leo
Oct 4	Virgo	Jul 23	Virgo	Sep 7	Virgo
Oct 29	Libra	Aug 17	Libra	Oct 1	Libra
Nov 23	Scorpio	Sep 12	Scorpio	Oct 25	Scorpio
Dec 17	Sagittarius	Oct 8	Sagittarius	Nov 18	Sagittarius
		Nov 5	Capricorn	Dec 12	Capricorn
		Dec 9	Aquarius		

(CONTINUED)

1991		1992		1993	
Jan 1	Capricorn	Jan 1	Sagittarius	Jan 1	Aquarius
Jan 5	Aquarius	Jan 25	Capricorn	Jan 3	Pisces
Jan 28	Pisces	Feb 18	Aquarius	Feb 2	Aries
Feb 22	Aries	Mar 13	Pisces	Jun 6	Taurus
Mar 18	Taurus	Apr 7	Aries	Jul 5	Gemini
Apr 12	Gemini	May 1	Taurus	Aug 1	Cancer
May 8	Cancer	May 25	Gemini	Aug 27	Leo
Jun 5	Leo	Jun 19	Cancer	Sep 21	Virgo
Jul 11	Virgo	Jul 13	Leo	Oct 15	Libra
Aug 21	Leo	Aug 7	Virgo	Nov 8	Scorpio
Oct 6	Virgo	Aug 31	Libra	Dec 2	Sagittarius
Nov 9	Libra	Sep 24	Scorpio	Dec 26	Capricorn
Dec 6	Scorpio	Oct 19	Sagittarius		
Dec 31	Sagittarius	Nov 13	Capricorn		
		Dec 8	Aquarius		

1994		1995		1996	
Jan 19	Aquarius	Jan 1	Scorpio	Jan 1	Aquarius
Feb 12	Pisces	Jan 7	Sagittarius	Jan 14	Pisces
Mar 8	Aries	Feb 4	Capricorn	Feb 8	Aries
Apr 1	Taurus	Mar 2	Aquarius	Mar 5	Taurus
Apr 26	Gemini	Mar 28	Pisces	Apr 3	Gemini
May 20	Cancer	Apr 21	Aries	Aug 7	Cancer
Jun 15	Leo	May 16	Taurus	Sep 7	Leo
Jul 11	Virgo	Jun 10	Gemini	Oct 3	Virgo
Aug 7	Libra	Jul 5	Cancer	Oct 29	Libra
Sep 7	Scorpio	Jul 29	Leo	Nov 22	Scorpio

1994		1995		1996	
		Aug 22	Virgo	Dec 17	Sagittarius
		Sep 16	Libra		
		Oct 10	Scorpio		
		Nov 3	Sagittarius		
		Nov 27	Capricorn		
		Dec 21	Aquarius		
1997		**1998**		**1999**	
Jan 1	Sagittarius	Jan 1	Aquarius	Jan 1	Capricorn
Jan 10	Capricorn	Jan 9	Capricorn	Jan 4	Aquarius
Feb 2	Aquarius	Mar 4	Aquarius	Jan 28	Pisces
Feb 26	Pisces	Apr 6	Pisces	Feb 21	Aries
Mar 23	Aries	May 3	Aries	Mar 18	Taurus
Apr 16	Taurus	May 29	Taurus	Apr 12	Gemini
May 10	Gemini	Jun 24	Gemini	May 8	Cancer
Jun 3	Cancer	Jul 19	Cancer	Jun 5	Leo
Jun 28	Leo	Aug 13	Leo	Jul 12	Virgo
Jul 23	Virgo	Sep 6	Virgo	Aug 15	Leo
Aug 17	Libra	Sep 30	Libra	Oct 7	Virgo
Sep 11	Scorpio	Oct 24	Scorpio	Nov 8	Libra
Oct 8	Sagittarius	Nov 17	Sagittarius	Dec 5	Scorpio
Nov 5	Capricorn	Dec 11	Capricorn	Dec 30	Sagittarius
Dec 11	Aquarius				

(CONTINUED)

2000		2001		2002	
Jan 1	Sagittarius	Jan 1	Aquarius	Jan 1	Capricorn
Jan 24	Capricorn	Jan 3	Pisces	Jan 18	Aquarius
Feb 17	Aquarius	Feb 2	Aries	Feb 11	Pisces
Mar 13	Pisces	Jun 6	Taurus	Mar 7	Aries
Apr 6	Aries	Jul 5	Gemini	Apr 1	Taurus
Apr 30	Taurus	Aug 1	Cancer	Apr 25	Gemini
May 25	Gemini	Aug 26	Leo	May 20	Cancer
Jun 18	Cancer	Sep 20	Virgo	Jun 14	Leo
Jul 13	Leo	Oct 15	Libra	Jul 10	Virgo
Aug 6	Virgo	Nov 8	Scorpio	Aug 7	Libra
Aug 30	Libra	Dec 2	Sagittarius	Sep 7	Scorpio
Sep 24	Scorpio	Dec 26	Capricorn		
Oct 19	Sagittarius				
Nov 12	Capricorn				
Dec 8	Aquarius				

2003		2004		2005	
Jan 1	Scorpio	Jan 1	Aquarius	Jan 1	Sagittarius
Jan 7	Sagittarius	Jan 14	Pisces	Jan 9	Capricorn
Feb 4	Capricorn	Feb 8	Aries	Feb 2	Aquarius
Mar 2	Aquarius	Mar 5	Taurus	Feb 26	Pisces
Mar 27	Pisces	Apr 3	Gemini	Mar 22	Aries
Apr 21	Aries	Aug 7	Cancer	Apr 15	Taurus
May 16	Taurus	Sep 6	Leo	May 9	Gemini
Jun 9	Gemini	Oct 3	Virgo	Jun 3	Cancer
Jul 4	Cancer	Oct 28	Libra	Jun 28	Leo
Jul 28	Leo	Nov 22	Scorpio	Jul 22	Virgo

2003		2004		2005	
Aug 22	Libra	Dec 16	Sagittarius	Aug 16	Libra
Sep 15	Virgo			Sep 11	Scorpio
Oct 9	Scorpio			Oct 7	Sagittarius
Nov 2	Sagittarius			Nov 5	Capricorn
Nov 26	Capricorn			Dec 15	Aquarius
Dec 21	Aquarius				

2006		2007		2008	
Jan 1	Aquarius	Jan 1	Capricorn	Jan 1	Sagittarius
Mar 5	Capricorn	Jan 3	Aquarius	Jan 24	Capricorn
Apr 5	Pisces	Jan 27	Pisces	Feb 17	Aquarius
May 3	Aries	Feb 21	Aries	Mar 12	Pisces
May 29	Taurus	Mar 17	Taurus	Apr 6	Aries
Jun 23	Gemini	Apr 11	Gemini	Apr 30	Taurus
Jul 18	Cancer	May 8	Cancer	May 24	Gemini
Aug 12	Leo	Jun 5	Leo	Jun 18	Cancer
Sep 6	Virgo	Jul 14	Virgo	Jul 12	Leo
Sep 30	Libra	Aug 8	Leo	Aug 5	Virgo
Oct 24	Scorpio	Oct 8	Virgo	Aug 30	Libra
Nov 17	Sagittarius	Nov 8	Libra	Sep 23	Scorpio
Dec 11	Capricorn	Dec 5	Scorpio	Oct 18	Sagittarius
		Dec 30	Sagittarius	Nov 12	Capricorn
				Dec 7	Aquarius

(CONTINUED)

2009		2010		2011	
Jan 1	Aquarius	Jan 1	Capricorn	Jan 1	Scorpio
Jan 3	Pisces	Jan 18	Aquarius	Jan 7	Sagittarius
Feb 2	Aries	Feb 11	Pisces	Feb 4	Capricorn
Apr 11	Pisces	Mar 7	Aries	Mar 1	Aquarius
Apr 24	Aries	Mar 31	Taurus	Mar 27	Pisces
Jun 6	Taurus	Apr 25	Gemini	Apr 20	Aries
Jul 5	Gemini	May 19	Cancer	May 15	Taurus
Jul 31	Cancer	Jun 14	Leo	Jun 9	Gemini
Aug 26	Leo	Jul 10	Virgo	Jul 3	Cancer
Sep 20	Virgo	Aug 6	Libra	Jul 28	Leo
Oct 14	Libra	Sep 8	Scorpio	Aug 21	Virgo
Nov 7	Scorpio	Nov 7	Libra	Sep 14	Libra
Dec 1	Sagittarius	Nov 29	Scorpio	Oct 9	Scorpio
Dec 25	Capricorn			Nov 2	Sagittarius
				Nov 26	Capricorn
				Dec 20	Aquarius

2012		2013		2014	
Jan 1	Aquarius	Jan 1	Sagittarius	Jan 1	Capricorn
Jan 14	Pisces	Jan 8	Capricorn	Mar 5	Aquarius
Feb 8	Aries	Feb 1	Aquarius	Apr 5	Pisces
Mar 5	Taurus	Feb 25	Pisces	May 2	Aries
Apr 3	Gemini	Mar 21	Aries	May 28	Taurus
Aug 7	Cancer	Apr 15	Taurus	Jun 23	Gemini
Sep 6	Leo	May 9	Gemini	Jul 18	Cancer
Oct 3	Virgo	Jun 2	Cancer	Aug 12	Leo
Oct 28	Libra	Jun 27	Leo	Sep 5	Virgo

2012		2013		2014	
Nov 21	Scorpio	Jul 22	Virgo	Sep 29	Libra
Dec 15	Sagittarius	Aug 16	Libra	Oct 23	Scorpio
		Sep 11	Scorpio	Nov 16	Sagittarius
		Oct 7	Sagittarius	Dec 10	Capricorn
		Nov 5	Capricorn		

2015		2016		2017	
Jan 1	Capricorn	Jan 1	Sagittarius	Jan 1	Aquarius
Jan 3	Aquarius	Jan 23	Capricorn	Jan 3	Pisces
Jan 27	Pisces	Feb 16	Aquarius	Feb 3	Aries
Feb 20	Aries	Mar 12	Pisces	Apr 2	Pisces
Mar 17	Taurus	Apr 5	Aries	Apr 28	Aries
Apr 11	Gemini	Apr 29	Taurus	Jun 6	Taurus
May 7	Cancer	May 24	Gemini	Jul 4	Gemini
Jun 5	Leo	Jun 17	Cancer	Jul 31	Cancer
Jul 18	Virgo	Jul 12	Leo	Aug 25	Leo
Jul 31	Leo	Aug 5	Virgo	Sep 19	Virgo
Oct 8	Virgo	Aug 29	Libra	Oct 14	Libra
Nov 8	Libra	Sep 23	Scorpio	Nov 7	Scorpio
Dec 4	Scorpio	Oct 18	Sagittarius	Dec 1	Sagittarius
Dec 30	Sagittarius	Nov 11	Capricorn	Dec 25	Capricorn
		Dec 7	Aquarius		

Appendix B

JUPITER IN THE SIGNS 1925–2017			
1/1/1925	Capricorn	5/12/1939	Aries
1/7/1926	Aquarius	10/31/1939	Pisces
1/19/1927	Pisces	12/21/1939	Aries
6/7/1927	Aries	5/17/1940	Taurus
9/12/1927	Pisces	5/2/1941	Gemini
1/28/1928	Aries	6/11/1942	Cancer
6/5/1928	Taurus	7/1/1943	Leo
6/13/1929	Gemini	7/24/1944	Virgo
6/27/1930	Cancer	8/26/1945	Libra
7/18/1931	Leo	9/26/1946	Scorpio
8/12/1932	Virgo	10/25/1947	Sagittarius
9/1/1933	Libra	11/16/1948	Capricorn
10/12/1934	Scorpio	4/13/1949	Aquarius
11/10/1935	Sagittarius	6/28/1949	Capricorn
12/3/1936	Capricorn	12/1/1949	Aquarius
12/20/1937	Aquarius	4/16/1950	Pisces
5/15/1938	Pisces	9/16/1950	Aquarius
7/31/1938	Aquarius	12/2/1950	Pisces
12/30/1938	Pisces	4/22/1951	Aries

(CONTINUED)

4/29/1952	Taurus
5/10/1953	Gemini
5/25/1954	Cancer
6/14/1955	Leo
11/18/1955	Virgo
1/19/1956	Leo
7/8/1956	Virgo
12/14/1956	Libra
2/20/1957	Virgo
8/8/1957	Libra
1/14/1958	Scorpio
3/21/1958	Libra
9/8/1958	Scorpio
2/11/1959	Sagittarius
4/25/1959	Scorpio
10/6/1959	Sagittarius
3/2/1960	Capricorn
6/11/1960	Sagittarius
10/27/1960	Capricorn
3/16/1961	Aquarius
8/13/1961	Capricorn
11/5/1961	Aquarius
3/26/1962	Pisces
4/5/1963	Aries
4/13/1964	Taurus
4/22/1965	Gemini
9/22/1965	Cancer
11/18/1965	Gemini
5/6/1966	Cancer
9/28/1966	Leo
1/17/1967	Cancer
5/24/1967	Leo
10/20/1967	Virgo
2/28/1968	Leo
6/16/1968	Virgo
11/16/1968	Libra
3/31/1969	Virgo
7/16/1969	Libra
12/17/1969	Scorpio
5/1/1970	Libra
8/16/1970	Scorpio
1/15/1971	Sagittarius
6/6/1971	Scorpio
9/12/1971	Sagittarius
2/7/1972	Capricorn
7/25/1972	Sagittarius
9/26/1972	Capricorn
2/24/1973	Aquarius
3/8/1974	Pisces
3/19/1975	Aries
3/27/1976	Taurus
8/24/1976	Gemini
10/17/1976	Taurus
4/2/1977	Gemini
8/21/1977	Cancer
12/31/1977	Gemini
4/13/1978	Cancer
9/6/1978	Leo

3/1/1979	Cancer
4/21/1979	Leo
9/30/1979	Virgo
10/28/1980	Libra
11/28/1981	Scorpio
12/2/1982	Sagittarius
1/20/1984	Capricorn
2/7/1985	Aquarius
2/21/1986	Pisces
3/3/1987	Aries
3/9/1988	Taurus
7/22/1988	Gemini
12/1/1988	Taurus
3/12/1989	Gemini
7/31/1989	Cancer
8/19/1990	Leo
9/13/1991	Virgo
10/11/1992	Libra
11/11/1993	Scorpio
12/13/1994	Sagittarius
1/4/1996	Capricorn
1/22/1997	Aquarius
2/5/1998	Pisces
2/14/1999	Aries
6/29/1999	Taurus
7/1/2000	Gemini
7/12/2001	Cancer
8/2/2002	Leo
8/28/2003	Virgo
9/26/2004	Libra
10/27/2005	Scorpio
11/25/2006	Sagittarius
12/19/2007	Capricorn
1/6/2009	Aquarius
1/19/2010	Pisces
6/7/2010	Aries
9/10/2010	Pisces
1/23/2011	Aries
6/5/2011	Taurus
6/12/2012	Gemini
6/27/2013	Cancer
7/17/2014	Leo
8/12/2015	Virgo
9/10/2016	Libra
10/11/2017	Scorpio
11/9/2018	Sagittarius

Appendix C

SATURN IN THE SIGNS 1925–2017			
1/1/1925	Scorpio	4/4/1949	Leo
12/2/1926	Sagittarius	5/30/1949	Virgo
3/16/1929	Capricorn	11/21/1950	Libra
5/4/1929	Sagittarius	3/8/1951	Virgo
12/1/1929	Capricorn	8/14/1951	Libra
2/25/1932	Aquarius	10/23/1953	Scorpio
8/14/1932	Capricorn	1/13/1956	Sagittarius
11/21/1932	Aquarius	5/13/1956	Scorpio
2/15/1935	Pisces	10/11/1956	Sagittarius
4/26/1937	Aries	1/6/1959	Capricorn
10/19/1937	Pisces	1/4/1962	Aquarius
1/15/1938	Aries	3/25/1964	Pisces
7/7/1939	Taurus	9/17/1964	Aquarius
9/23/1939	Aries	12/17/1964	Pisces
3/21/1940	Taurus	3/4/1967	Aries
5/9/1942	Gemini	4/30/1969	Taurus
6/21/1944	Cancer	6/19/1971	Gemini
8/3/1946	Leo	1/11/1972	Taurus
9/29/1948	Virgo	2/22/1972	Gemini

(CONTINUED)

8/2/1972	Cancer
1/8/1974	Gemini
4/19/1974	Cancer
9/18/1975	Leo
1/15/1976	Cancer
6/6/1976	Leo
11/18/1977	Virgo
1/6/1978	Leo
7/27/1978	Virgo
9/22/1980	Libra
11/30/1982	Scorpio
5/7/1983	Libra
8/25/1983	Scorpio
11/18/1985	Sagittarius
2/14/1988	Capricorn
6/1/1988	Sagittarius
11/13/1988	Capricorn
2/7/1991	Aquarius
5/22/1993	Pisces
7/1/1993	Aquarius
1/29/1994	Pisces
4/8/1996	Aries
6/10/1998	Taurus
10/26/1998	Aries
3/2/1999	Taurus
8/10/2000	Gemini
10/17/2000	Taurus
4/21/2001	Gemini
6/5/2003	Cancer
7/17/2005	Leo
9/3/2007	Virgo
10/30/2009	Libra
4/8/2010	Virgo
7/22/2010	Libra
10/6/2012	Scorpio
12/24/2014	Sagittarius
6/16/2015	Scorpio
9/19/2015	Sagittarius
12/21/2017	Capricorn

Sources

Part One: Examining Luck

The Freud Reader, edited by Peter Gay, New York: W. W. Norton & Company, 1989.

Chapter 1: Luck Begins

Nicholas Rescher. *Luck: The Brilliant Randomness of Everyday Life.* New York: Farrar, Straus & Giroux, 1995.

Dictionary.com

Americangaming.org

Chapter 2: Luck in Our Own Backyard

Jackson Lears. *Something for Nothing: Luck in America.* New York: Viking, 2003.

Kathryn Shanley. "Lady Luck or Mother Earth? Gaming as a Trope in Plains Indian Cultural Traditions," *Wicazo Sa Review* 15, no. 2 (Fall 2000): 93–101.

Alessandra Stanley. "In Battle for Bucks, Personality Beats Intellect." *New York Times,* October 13, 2006.

Angelfire.com

Luckymojo.com

45thdivisionmuseum.com

Navajo-arts.com

Collectorsguide.com

Astro.com (transcript, "Towards a Post-Modern Astrology" by Robert Hand)
Altreligion.about.com
Vcnevada.com
Imdb.com
Filmsandtv.com
91stbombgroup.com

Chapter 3: Luck and the Natural World

Jo Forty. *Mythology: A Visual Encyclopedia.* London: PRC Publications, Ltd., 1999.
Bill Harris. *The Good Luck Book: An A-to-Z Guide to Charms and Symbols.* New York: Ottenheimer Publishers, 1996.
Man-Ho Kwok and Joanne O'Brien. *The Elements of Feng Shui.* New York: Barnes & Noble Books, 1996.
Kirsten M. Lagatree. *Feng Shui: Arranging Your Home to Change Your Life.* New York: Villard, 1996.
Julia Lorusso and Joel Glick. *Healing Stones: The Therapeutic Use of Gems and Minerals.* Albuquerque: Brotherhood of Life Publishing, 1996.
Uma Silbey. *The Complete Crystal Guidebook.* New York: Bantam Books, 1996.
Vivien Sung. *Five-fold Happiness: Chinese Concepts of Luck, Prosperity, Longevity, Happiness and Wealth.* Chronical Books, 2002.
Barbara G. Walker. *The Woman's Dictionary of Symbols and Sacred Objects.* New York: HarperSanFrancisco, 1998.
Bartleby.com
Luckfactory.com
Artvision-viroqua.com
Amusingfacts.com
Tang.skidmore.edu
City.hitachi.ibaraki.jp
Historicimpressions.com

Bellaonline.com
Alohafriends.com
Crystal-cure.com
Fengshui.stellarweb.biz
Wofs.com
Cedarseed.com
Liasiagallery.com
Silvercrowcreations.com

Chapter 4: The Future of Luck Through Divination

Benson Brobick. *The Fated Sky: Astrology in History.* New York: Simon & Schuster, 2005.

Anistatia R. Miller and Jared M. Brown. *The Complete Astrological Handbook for the Twenty-First Century: Understanding and Combining the Wisdom of Chinese, Tibetan, Vedic, Arabian, Judaic, and Western Astrology.* New York: Schocken Books, 1999.

Reading Tea Leaves by a Highland Seer. New York: Clarkson Potter, 1995.

Gergory Whincup. *Rediscovering the I Ching.* New York: St. Martin's Griffen Group, 1996.

Peter Whitfield. *Astrology: A History.* New York: Harry N. Abrams, 2001.

Hellmut Wilhelm, translated by Cary F. Baynes. *The I Ching or Book of Changes.* Princeton, N.J.: Princeton University Press, 1950.

Chapter 5: Luck Through the Meaning of Numbers

Carlo Arancio. *La Vera Smorfia: Tutti I Numeri Da Giocae Al Lotto.* DVE Italia S.P.A., 1997.

John Bartlett. *Familiar Quotations.* Boston: Little, Brown and Company, 1955.

Jonathan Cott. *Thirteen: A Journey into the Number.* New York: Doubleday, 1996.

John King. *The Modern Numerology.* London: Blanford, 1996.
Annemarie Schimmel. *The Mystery of Numbers.* Oxford: Oxford University Press, 1993.
"Thais Pay Big Money for 'Lucky' License Plates," *Milwaukee Journal Sentinel,* August 31, 2003.

Chapter 6: Probable Luck, Reasonable Luck, Mathematician's Luck

Peter L. Bernstein. *Against the Gods: The Remarkable Story of Risk.* New York: John Wiley & Sons, Inc., 1998.
Michael Kaplan and Ellen Kaplan. *Chances Are: Adventures in Probability.* New York: Viking, 2006.
The Oxford Dictionary of Quotations. Oxford: Oxford University Press, 1980.
Nylottery.org

Chapter 7: Gambling: Sheer Games of Luck

John Bartlett. *Familiar Quotations.* Boston: Little, Brown and Company, 1955.
Peter L. Bernstein. *Against the Gods: The Remarkable Story of Risk.* New York: John Wiley and Sons, 1996.
Clint Brookhart. *Go Figure: Using Math to Answer Everyday Imponderables.* Chicago: Contemporary Books, 1998.
Fyodor Dostoyevsky. *The Gambler.* New York: Dover Publications, 1996.
Americangaming.org
Powerball.com
Nylottery.org
Calottery.com
Interlotto.com
Equine-world.co.uk
Jockeyclub.com

Nyra.com
Gaming.unlv.edu

Chapter 8: The Modern and Wacky World of Luck

John Bartlett. *Familiar Quotations.* Boston: Little, Brown and Company, 1955.

Phil Hellmuth Jr. *Bad Beats and Lucky Draws: Poker Strategies, Winning Hands, and Stories from the Professional Poker Tour.* New York: HarperCollins, 2004.

Esquire.com

DoylesRoom.com

Authorsden.com

Eddie Bennett obituary, *New York Times,* January 17, 1935.

Chairman's Letter, Berkshire Hathaway Annual Report, 2002.

Cnnsi.com and BabeRuth.com

Profootballhof.com

Clemson.edu

RandomHouse.com

Tiger Woods Press Conference: The Masters, April 9, 2002, at TigerWoods.com.

GolfDigest.com

Powerball.com

IGT.com

DoyleBrunson.com

FullTiltPoker.com

Chanpoker.com

Quotationspage.com

Archives.Gov. Geselbracht, Raymond H., "Harry Truman, Poker Player," *Prologue* 35, no.1 (Spring 2003).

Anecdotage.com

Abc.net.au. Margaret El-Chami, "Woody Allen's Luck," February 15, 2006.

Bartleby.com

Yale.edu
Harvard.edu
Brown.edu
Dartmouth.edu

Part Two: Personal Luck Profile

John Bartlett. *Familiar Quotations.* Boston: Little, Brown and Company, 1955.

Sir Wallis Budge. *Amulets and Talismans.* New York: Carol Publishing, 1992.

Scott Cunningham. *Cunningham's Encyclopedia of Magical Herbs.* St. Paul: Llewellyn Publications, 1993.

Scott Cunningham. *Magical Herbalism.* St. Paul: Llewellyn Publications, 1982.

Rosemary Gong. *Good Luck Life: The Essential Guide to Chinese American Celebrations and Culture.* New York: HarperResource, 2005.

Mark Gruner and Christopher K. Brown. *Mark Gruner's Numbers of Life: An Introduction to Numerology.* New York: Taplinger Publishing, 1978.

Julia Line. *Discover Numerology: Understanding and Using the Power of Numbers.* New York: Sterling Publishing, 1985.

Zolar's Magick of Color: Use the Power of Color to Transform Your Luck, Prosperity or Romance. New York: Fireside Books, 1994.

Bartleby.com

About the Authors

BARRIE DOLNICK is the author of twelve books. She works as a consultant and astrologer and teaches metaphysical concepts to the general public.

ANTHONY H. DAVIDSON is an attorney and has been studying luck and its effects on risk taking for the past several years.